A Garland Series

The Life & Times of Seven Major British Writers

Dryden
Pope
Swift
Richardson
Sterne
Johnson
Gibbon

A collection of 370 titles printed in photo-facsimile in 147 volumes

SWIFTIANA IV

On the Drapier's Letters, etc.
1724

Garland Publishing, Inc., New York & London

1975

Library of Congress Cataloging in Publication Data
Main entry under title:

On the Drapier's letters, etc., 1724.

(Swiftiana ; 4) (The Life & times of seven major British writers)

Reprint of A word or two to the people of Ireland concerning the brass money that is, and shall be coin'd by Mr. Woods, and which he is endeavouring to impose upon us, printed by J. Harding, Dublin, 1724; of Some farther account of the original disputes in Ireland, about farthings and halfpence, in a discourse with a Quaker of Dublin, printed in 1724; of Some reasons shewing the necessity the people of Ireland are under, for continuing to refuse Mr. Wood's coinage, by D. Bindon, printed in Dublin, 1724; of Remarks upon Mr. Wood's coyn and proceedings, by Sir M. Creagh, printed by W. Wilmot, Dublin, 1724; of A letter to M. B. Drapier, printed in Dublin, 1724; of A letter from a young lady, to the Revd. D--n S--t, printed in 1724; and of The present state of Ireland consider'd in a letter to the Revd. Dean Swift, by a true patriot, printed in 1724.

1. Money--Ireland--History--Sources. 2. Coinage--Ireland--Sources. I. Series.
PR3726.S95 vol. 4 [HG950.I8] 828'.5'09s
ISBN 0-8240-1265-8 [332.4'9415] 75-44187

Printed in the United States of America

Contents

A word or two to the people of Ireland,...

Some farther account of the original disputes in Ireland,...

Bindon, David. *Some reasons shewing the necessity the people of Ireland are under,...*

Creagh, Sir Michael. *Remarks upon Mr. Wood's coyn.*

A letter to M. B. Drapier.

A letter from a young lady, to the Revd. D--n S--t.

The present state of Ireland consider'd.

A WORD OR TWO

Bibliographical note:

this facsimile has been made from a copy in the Beinecke Library of Yale University (NZ.724w)

A

Word or Two

TO THE

People of Ireland,

CONCERNING

The Braſs Money that is, and ſhall be Coin'd by Mr. WOODS, and which he is endeavouring to Impoſe upon Us.

By a Well-wiſher to his Country.

DUBLIN:

Printed by *John Harding* in *Moleſworth*'s-*Court* in *Fiſhamble Street*.

Salus Populi, Suprema Lex est.

AS every honest Man is inflam'd with a Love to his Native Country, and has his Heart fill'd with the best Wishes for its Welfare, so it must be thought every ones Duty to promote this great End, and this innate Passion will shew it self in every Action of our Lives that has a Tendency this Way. Who can in such a Critical Juncture as this, which demands all our Thoughts, sit still as an unconcerned Spectator, when we are threatned with utter Ruin from this accursed Seheme of *Woods*'s? I hope by this Time we are all sensible of the Miserable Consequences this Project, should it take, will involve us in, which are enumerated in Mr. B. the Drapier's two Letters, which I don't doubt have been carefully perus'd by *all* in this City, and if some Pains and Care be taken will ſoon make their Way thro' this Kingdom. Surely this Dealer in Droſs, muſt not only be doting, but daring to a Degree, that is endeavouring to Impoſe his TRASH upon us, contrary to the Repreſentation of our Honourable Houſe of Commons preſented in the moſt humble Manner to his Majeſty, and the Voice of the whole Nation to a Man, and they ſay; *Vox Populi, Vox Dei.* There may be a few concerned with him in this Work of Iniquity, whom I don't think worth the Naming being Men abondoned by their Country; which they are endeavouring to ruin, and of the moſt deſperate Fortunes, tho' they would wake us believe ſtrange Things of Copper Mines, and the Lord knows what; theſe Men I ſay are at Work to raiſe themſelves thus, relinquiſhing all the Methods of honeſt Gain, willing to give up all their Hopes of a Future Happineſs it ſelf, provided they may but ſuc-

ceed

ceed in their present wicked Design against us. As they are Men who have nothing to loose, if their Scheme should not succeed, so they will be for ever enriched by it, should it take. They are indeed much upon the same Foot with *Buccaneers*, *No Purchase*, *No Pay*. What abandon'd Wretches must these be that are thus aiming to rear themselves on the Destruction of their fellow Creatures, for I will not say Countrymen, worse than the Savage Canibals, who deprive us only of our Lives, and so put an end with it to all our Miseries at least in this World; but those are for devouring our Substance, and thereby expose us to all the Calamities that a Life of Poverty can be attended with; like Rats, they are Night and Day nibling at our Destruction; they are hanging out their baits by spacious Proposals to allure us, but I hope we are by this Time on our Guard, that the Watch Word is gone about, that their

their wicked Intentions againſt us may not prevail. If I had it in my Power, it ſhould be writ over all our Church Doors in Capital Letters, *Let none Pollute this Holy Place by entering it, that takes or receives any of* Woods's *Braſs Money*; that if there ſhould be any among us ſtill infatuated in Favour of either the Man or his Coin, they might be deprived of all the Benefits of a Religious Aſſembly, as *Traitors* to their Country, and the *Betrayers* of it. But perhaps ſome may think this Puniſhment too ſevere, let ſuch a one Conſider that if he ſhould happen to call a Woman a Whore, and the Spiritual Court gets hold of him, he muſt run thro' all the Forms of that Court, and looſe both his Money, and his Breath, before he can get clear of it, tho' in truth the Woman may be as arrant a Whore, as ever was; now if the Difference of the Crimes be juſtly conſidered, the Objection to the Severity of the Puniſh-

Puniſhment will be anſwered. If *Cain* for the Death of his Brother *Abel* was Sentenc'd by his Maker to be a Fugitive and a Vagabond in the Earth, does not *Woods* and his Accomplices richly deſerve the ſame Fate, and I wou'd too with him they were mark'd, leaſt any finding them ſhou'd Kill them. But yet I truſt that our Ruin is not ſo near, as they wou'd make us believe, and this I will endeavour to evince in the following Particulars, and in the firſt Place, We are aſſured that His Majeſty in his Patent to *Woods* has not obliged us to take his *Half-pence*; ſo that it is entirely left to our own Option to take or refuſe them as we ſee Good; it lies in our own Breaſts, and there is not one Syllable, from Beginning to End of the Patent forcing or compelling us to take them. If his Majeſty has been ſo gracious to us herein, where is the Man, or who is he, that is for forcing this Traſh upon us, why truely

Mr.

Mr. *Woods* the little domineering Tyrant, for he deserves no better Name that would impose on a whole Kingdom without either Rhime or Reason. *2dly*, These *Half-pence* are not made Current by any Law, and as his Majesty has left us to our Liberty herein, so the Currency of them cannot obtain, unless we will our selves, till a Proclamation be issued out to this Effect, which brings me to the 3d Particular, That our Laws, as we are assur'd, do not oblige any Person to take or receive any other Money than *Gold* and *Silver*, and that in Consequence hereof, his Majesty cannot be suppos'd to issue a Proclamation against Law, and if this shou'd happen to be done by Mistake, we are not oblig'd to comply with it, because it wou'd be Void in it self as contrary to the Laws of the Land, I may likewise add to the Law of Nature, which provides for the Safety and Welfare of Mankind: But if these *Half-pence* pass,

One

One Million and a Half of People must be ruin'd. Another Thing that I would consider in order to remove our Fears, is that his Majesty's Interest in this Kingdom will suffer very much, if this Project of *Woods*'s takes. What Jealousies and Fears has it not already rais'd in the Breasts of many of his best Subjects, and what disaffection and Confusion will not follow, if it succeeds! I don't think it may be amiss to reflect on what *Hudibrass* has long since told us, that,

> *Hard Words, Jealousies and Fears,*
> *Set Folks together by the Ears.*

I am sure the *Protestants* of this Kingdom have never come behind his Majesty's best Subjects in their affectionate Zeal for his Royal Person and Government; they have on every Occasion given the most convincing Proofs of their Readiness to serve him. For these and the like Reasons they can't think of being abandon'd at this Juncture, or given

up

up to the Power of One or Many. We think we have a Right to claim the Protection of his Majesty and the English Nation as their Brethren, united by the same Happy Constitution, Born under the same excellent Laws, and Subjects to the same most Gracious Monarch, our common Head and Father.

By a late Paragraph of *Woods*'s, which I saw in the *English* Prints, and his persisting in his Design against us, notwithstanding the Opposition it has so generally met with, I mean from this Kingdom, I can't but think that he may be endeavouring to Represent us as a Disobedient and Disaffectionate People to his Majesty, the better to introduce his Counterfeit Species among us. But let us fear nothing from this Quarter, our Actions and Services will shew us the contrary, notwithstanding all the Artifice and Tricks us'd by *Woods* on this Occasion. I am glad to see so good a Spirit rais'd against him and his

his Scheme, which I ſhould be ſorry to ſee Flag, till this Impending Cloud is blown over. We are told of a very good Law that obtain'd among the *Sybarites*, an Antient People of *Italy*. That whoever propos'd any Alteration to be made (and ſure this of Mr. *Woods*'s is One, and a very deſtructive one too) ſhould ſtep out and do it with a Rope about his Neck; if the Matter propos'd was Generally approved, then it ſhou'd paſs into a *Law*, but if not, the Propoſer to be immediately Hang'd. I don't doubt but the Reader will be making the Application in his own Thoughts; and one need not be Maſter of much Magick to know which Way. If this Law had been a Part of our Conſtitution as it was of the *Sybarites*, I can't help thinking that we ſhou'd not have heard either of Mr. *Woods* or his Coyn, or he wou'd then it may be have paid a Deference to the Opinion of our People, nay for what I know he wou'd have made a Contract

with

with us instead of some others. As he has taken upon him to Misrepresent our Circumstances to his Majesty, what Punishment may be due to him by Law, he wou'd do well to consider. If he has in Justice Forfeited his Patent, by his not conforming to the Terms of it, as I have heard some People alledge, then we are to look upon him as depriv'd of all his Power, even the very Semblance of it, by which he has heretofore wrought so powerfully on our Fears; and who knows but he may, with the *Bees* drop his *Sting* and *Life* together. No Body will think this a hard Insinuation, if they consider Mr. *Woods*, as indeed they should : Our Enemy, a Man engag'd in a Scheme, the most Destructive to this Kingdom that perhaps was ever Projected. Whether he has been the former of it himself, or may beholden to others more High and Mighty than we imagine, I cant tell, his Puissant Confederates, if he has any, are still behind the

the Curtain, and the time is not yet come for their throwing off the Mask; He only thinks fit to tread the Stage as their great *Goliah*, but who knows but he may meet with a *David* among us, who thus defies all our *Hosts*. Time which is the discoverer of all Hidden things, may perhaps unravel to us this whole Scene of Iniquity, so that were I one of his Accomplices, I would be for making a timely Retreat by delivering up Mr. *Woods* to the Justice and Resentments of an Abused Monarch and an Injured People. It's thought, had he been in any other Country, that he wou'd long since have met with a fate Suitable to his Demerits. Since the Writing of this, we have receiv'd a fresh Alarm of Forty thousand Pounds of these Half pence that are to be poured in upon Us; well admit there be, that his Majesty's Commissioners and Collectors do receive them, and the Army to be paid with them, what will all this Signifie to Us;

the

the Word of Safety has been given You, say but NO, be but steady to your Resolutions against receiving or Uttering this Trash, and Vigorous in Your Opposition and all will be well with You . Let who will take them you are not oblig'd to follow their Example, and since *Woods* himself has no Right to Compell you, who has ? Consider the Particulars I have before hinted at, and you need be under no fears, no Apprehensions; it lyes only in your own Breasts whether they shall Live or not. Let us to a Man follow our Leaders, I mean our Honourable House of Commons who have so Gloriously exerted themselves this last Session to Damn them, they are still in the same Mind, and I doubt not like minded, and as our Saviours will stand in the Gap to prevent our Destruction; They are the Guardians & Trustees of our Religious and Civil Liberties of every thing that is dear and Valuable to us both as Men and Christians, Let us not refuse

with

with one Hand, while we are Stretching out the Other. I have heard with great Pleasure, that a Certain Great Man among us has declared, that if these Half-pence of *Woods's* be legitimated here, that he will Resign all his Employments. To pass by that Vulgar objection, *that Great Men never Speak as they think*; I dont believe but this Gentleman is Sincere. Every One knows he has a very Considerable Stake in this Kingdom, and therefore must be one of the first Sufferers, shou'd this wicked Project succeed; So that not only his Interest, but his Country call upon him most loudly to Rescue us from all the Load we must otherways Sink under, and to take all the Methods he can possibly think of to baffle all attempts for our Ruin. I would have Every Man of what Rank or Degree soever he may be, that contributes at this Time to our Preservation, either by his Assistance or Advice, consider that he deserves not only Immortal Fame but

but if he ſhould miſs of this, he has ſtill behind the moſt Solid Satisfaction and Pleaſure that great and Virtuous Actions are always attended with; and ſuch a One may Expect that Future Generations will riſe up and call him *Bleſſed*. In this Let us all be of one Heart and one Mind, and no Diſtinction heard of among us, but who are for theſe Braſs Half-pence or againſt them, or in other Words, who are for or againſt their Country, and which is the moſt amiable Character, a PATRIOT or BETRAYER of it. Let us all joyn in our Prayers to Almighty God, for the Proſperity of thoſe who Love our Nation and are Friends to us; and that the Workers of Iniquity may be deſtroyed.

FINIS

SOME FARTHER ACCOUNT

Bibliographical note:

this facsimile has been made from a copy in the Beinecke Library of Yale University (Ik.D362.724s)

Some farther Account
OF THE
Original Disputes
IN
IRELAND,
ABOUT
Farthings and Halfpence.
IN A
DISCOURSE
WITH A
Quaker of Dublin.

Quærenda Pecunia primum.

Printed in the Year 1724.

Some farther Account

OF THE

Original Disputes

In *IRELAND*, &c.

I Need make no Apology for my Enquiries into this Affair, with one who was entirely a Stranger, seeing he was no Stranger to the Thing I enquir'd after: It is enough to say, that meeting with a sensible and intelligent Person, *one of the People call'd* QUAKERS, and who came lately from *Dublin*, and falling into an Acquaintance with him, he occasionally mention'd the Heats and Wrangling which they had very unhappily fallen into in *Ireland*, about the currency of the Copper-Money there.

I had indeed, a long time wiſh'd for ſuch an Opportunity to talk with ſomebody or other, on that Subject, for I always believ'd what I am now confirm'd in, *namely*, that we never had a true, or at beſt, not a full Account of that Mattter; and I that always lov'd to keep one Ear open, and if poſſible, to hear both Sides of a Queſtion, had for ſome time ſuſpended my Judgment in this Caſe, in hopes that I ſhou'd one time or other come to hear more of it.

In conſequence of this Reſerve of my Thoughts I told the honeſt QUAKER, I ſhou'd be very glad to have a full Account of that Affair, and ask'd him, if he had been acquainted with it? He gravely reply'd, Why truly I am well acquainted with it, Friend; but I find the People of *England* neither well acquainted with it, or willing to be inform'd: They are not all ſo, *ſaid I*, for I am very deſirous to be inform'd of it; and then I told him what I have ſaid above, of my ſo long wiſhing for a full Account, and believing we had not been well us'd in it before.

Truly Friend, *ſays he*, *thou* haſt judg'd rightly as to *thy* having heard but Part of this Story; but I fear *thy* Patience will not ſerve *thee* to hear the whole, for *verily* it will take up much Time, eſpecially in my ſlow Way of ſpeaking.

Well, I preſs'd him to give me a full Account of it, aſſuring him, that I had as much Patience as Curioſity; and that, *in a word*, I had ſo much Deſire to hear it, that I cou'd not want

Pati-

Patience, if it held all Night, deſiring him not to ſhorten any Part of it; upon which he undertook it, and began thus:

Firſt he told me, That he ſuppos'd the chief Information I had receiv'd of that Affair, was, from the Votes and Reſolves of the Parliament of *Ireland*, and their ſeveral Addreſſes to the King; *I told him,* It was ſo, including only two or three Letters, or Advertiſements, publiſh'd by way of Libel, or Pamphlet, in ſome of our publick Papers.

In truth, Friend, *ſays he,* I ſaw thoſe Papers too, but they ſeem'd to be written by ſome Hand as ignorant as officious; ſo that I ſhou'd almoſt think, thoſe which argued againſt the Copper-Money, were hir'd by the Adverſary to expoſe the Cauſe, and give Advantages againſt themſelves.

Well, *ſaid I,* but what ſay you to the Proceedings in the Parliament of *Ireland*?

As for that, *ſays he,* e'en let *thee* and I lay them aſide for the preſent; *verily,* they need not ſo much as be nam'd in the Caſe; neither ſhall I have any Occaſion *to ſpeak of them* in all my Diſcourſe, except only as *thou* ſeeſt I do now, *namely* to let *thee* know, that *I do not ſpeak of them.*

Thoſe Aſſemblies, *added he,* which *ye* call *Parliaments* are Numbers of Men call'd together by our Government, to make and amend Laws, redreſs the Grievances, and do divers Things which are needful to be done ; but they are compos'd of fallible Men, and I will not ſay they cannot Err, and be miſtaken, even in their Parliament Capacity ; whether they have been now miſtaken, or impos'd upon by ſubtle Men from Without-Doors, is not my preſent Buſineſs to ſay, or *thine* to enquire ; to which I gave a little *Hum*, with like Gravity, *and ſo he went on.*

He told me then, That I muſt therefore learn to diſtinguiſh, in this Affair, between what was done in Parliament, and what was done out of Parliament ; for indeed, *ſays he*, the Scheme of all this Matter was laid, and much tranſacted, before the Parliament came together, and conſequently what happen'd in Parliament, cou'd not be the Cauſe of what Oppoſition was reſolv'd on, becauſe then it muſt act before it had a Being ; whether what was done in Parliament, was an Effect conſequent to what went before ? *Of that, Friend*, ſaid he, *judge Thou.*

Nor, *ſays he*, have you in *England* been only miſtaken, by turning your Eyes to the Votes of Parliament, and to ſome fooliſh weak Papers, where one Part of the Fact is repreſented, and the other taken no Notice of ; by which means your Judgments are biaſs'd, and prepoſſeſs'd, in Favour of that which is moſt popular : But, *ſays he*, if I am not miſtaken, *thou* art, and the People here in *England* have been amus'd, and led quite beſide the Queſtion ; *ye* are taken up in diſcuſſing the Terms of the Grant ; calculating the Value of the New Coin ; the Profits of the Patentee ; and the

the Advantage, or Diſadvantage, which accrues to the Kingdom of *Ireland* by this Copper-Money; in all which Diſputes and Calculations, *adds my Friend*, the *Men of Art*, thy *Sons of Figures and Cyphers* are moſt extreamly wrong, as I may tell *thee* hereafter.

But there is, *adds he*, a previous Queſtion, which ſhou'd have been firſt determin'd; and that is *what the main Queſtion is?* for verily we are by no Means agreed about that yet, and 'till that is anſwer'd, all the reſt is beating the Air, and dancing in a Circle.

Why, *ſays I*, the main Queſtion (as I underſtand it) is, whether the Farthings and Halfpence are prejudicial, deſtructive, and dangerous to the People of *Ireland*, or whether they are not?

No, no, Friend, *ſays my* QUAKER, *thou* art miſtaken quite, that is a Queſtion, (and I may ſay ſomething to that alſo hereafter) but that is not the main Queſtion to be diſcuſs'd, or which was firſt diſcuſs'd among us, in order to come at a clear Underſtanding of this Matter.

Why, *ſaid I*, this was the Queſtion debated and reſolv'd in your Parliament.

I tell *thee*, *ſaid he ſomewhat peeviſhly*, I am not ſpeaking of the Parliament; I wou'd not have them ſo much as nam'd, or any-thing done by them, mention'd; I am ſearching deeper into this Wound than thoſe State Surgeons cou'd go, and enquiring into what was before their Sitting, *I mean in their laſt Sitting*; therefore let them be no more ſpoken of in it.

Well, *ſays I*, then the Queſtion muſt be, whether the People of *Ireland* are willing to receive theſe Farthings and Halfpence, or not; or whether they are illegally and arbitrarily impos'd upon them.

No, no, Friend, *ſays the* QUAKER, *thou* art ſtill out of the right Way, *thou* wilt never come at the Bottom of the Buſineſs, by theſe Enquiries; for in that the Patent will anſwer *thee*, and the People of *Ireland* will anſwer *thee* in the other: *Then he added with ſome Warmth*, The Farthings and Halfpence were not forc'd upon *us illegally*, or *arbitrarily*, for they were not forc'd upon *us* at-all: The Patent (or Grant) gave no Power to *impoſe them*; neither were WE in *Ireland* oblig'd to take one Ounce of them, unleſs we freely and willingly (and by our own Choice) agreed to take them. *On the contrary*, the People, *as they* extreamly wanted them, *ſo they* univerſally approv'd of them: I aſſure *thee*, I have not heard of one Gainſayer, or that offer'd to make the leaſt Complaint againſt them, 'till they had been current, and paſt as Current-money among us, for ſeveral Months.

What then is the Caſe, *ſaid I*, for you ſeem ſomething myſterious about it?

Why, the main Queſtion, *Friend*, *ſays he*, was, whether the Patent was rightly granted? And ſo the

the Quarrel was a Debate of Intereſt, and lay between *William Wood*, the preſent Patentee, and *ſome other Perſons*, who laid their Hands upon it, in their Imagination: This, I ſay, is the Debate, and may be ſtated thus, *viz.* Whether the Coinage of *Copper-Money, being very profitable in itſelf*, ſhou'd continue to the ſaid *William Wood*, to whom the King had granted it, or whether it wou'd not be much better to ſet him aſide, and get it for *our ſelves.*

Hum! ſaid I again, but who do you mean by *our ſelves ?*

Nay, *ſays the* QUAKER, but *thou* may'ſt not enquire too far into the Secrets of others, that is not right; howbeit, I may (perhaps) open ſome Part of the Matter unto *thee*, in the latter End of the Story ; for I do not ſay, that the Men have no Names, nor do I ſay, that their Names are not known alſo: But of that alſo in its Place.

I begin to underſtand you, Friend, *ſays I*, and if I am right, you would have us believe, that there was an original Deſign, or Conſpiracy, among a Sett of Perſons in *Ireland*; *in ſhort*, to ſupplant Mr. *Wood*, get his Patent ſet aſide, and afterward to get a Grant of it for themſelves.

Verily, *thou haſt ſaid*, *ſays the* QUAKER, but I did not tell *thee*, that I wou'd have *thee* believe me; for of what Conſequence is it to me, *Friend*, *ſays he*, when I talk to *thee* of theſe Things, whether *thou* believeſt me or no ?

Well,

Well, well, *ſays I*, I ſee you are ſearching it to the Bottom indeed; pray go on with your Story then, and I will not interrupt you any more with my Enquiries: So he went on indeed, in a ſurprizing Manner, *to me*; and by which I was fully convinc'd, that really we in *England* had all-along taken this Affair by the wrong Handle, had ſeen it in a falſe Light, and that indeed we knew nothing at-all of the Matter.

He then went on, I ſay, and repeating to me the general Satisfaction with which the People of *Ireland* (as he had ſaid before) firſt receiv'd the Farthings and Halfpence; *he told me*, they did receive them, as Things they had not only a good Opinion of, but as what they were in great Want of; that after the firſt News of the Grant, and that the Coining of them was in-hand, which was ſome time before they arriv'd, the People were very impatient for their coming, and often expreſs'd their Concern, leſt the Coinage ſhou'd not go forward; that this did not ariſe from the uſual Eagerneſs of People after Novelty, but from the real Want the Country was in of ſmall Money, for the Supply of petty Caſh, Exchange of larger Species, for buying Proviſions in ſmall Quantities, and for all the other Occaſions, in which ſmall Money is uſually made uſe of.

He told me, that as ſoon as the Copper-Money appear'd, it met with a general Approbation; the People took it with ſo free a Conſent, that it became univerſally current: There was no Objections

jections rais'd, either against its Figure, which was very beautiful, or the Workmanship, which was compleat, or the Value and Fineness of the Metal, which (it was well known) the Grant it self had provided for, and which in Appearance seem'd to be such as was reasonable, and duely proportion'd to the Nature of the thing, and to the Usage in other Parts of the King's Dominions, in like Cases.

It is true, *he said*, they were something LIGHTER than the *Farthings* and *Halfpence* in *England*, but then, *he added*, they were HEAVIER than the *Bodles* and *Baubees* in *Scotland*, and there was just Reasons to be given for the Difference in both; but, *says he*, of that I shall talk farther with *thee* hereafter.

Then he went on to tell me, that this general Approbation of the People continued a great-while; for verily *Friend*, *says he*, we very sensibly felt the Ease they were to us in Trade; the Shop-keepers (in particular) felt the Advantage in their Retail Business; and it was impossible we cou'd act against our Light, so as to complain of that which we so universally rejoic'd at: I say, *he affirm'd*, that this general Approbation of the People continued a great-while, and that even when Complaints began to be heard, they had not their Beginning among the trading Part of the Nation: Nay, *he told me, and bid me remark it*, that some of those very Persons, who afterwards appear'd to be concern'd most violently against the Copper-Farthings, *&c.* were for some time the most forward to approve of

them,

them, and applaud the Advantage, which accrued to the Publick by them; that they were Advocates on all publick Occasions for the Patentee; appear'd extreamly pleas'd that the Coin obtain'd so general a Currency in Trade, and that the People were so well satisfy'd with it; and, *says he in his rough Way*, whether they LY'D then, or since, they know best.

Well but, *says I*, art *thou* well satisfy'd, or can'st *thou* make it appear, that these Men did not change their Opinion, 'till, *as thou say'st*, they form'd a Conspiracy to supplant Mr. *Wood*'s Patent.

Nay, *Friend*, *says he*, *thou* dost not use me fairly now; for that is to put me upon the Proof of Hours and Minutes, when Things were done, which were done in the Dark; for as *thou* hast call'd it a *Conspiracy*, *(which I did not)* it must then be secret, and I cannot speak to Minutes; but 'tis enough to say, *First*, That those very Men did some time after raise Clamours, and bring evil Accusations against the Grant for *Farthings* and *Halfpence*, against the Coin itself, and against *thy* Friend, *William Wood*, the Patentee, to whom the Privilege is granted. And, *Secondly*, That some Persons have propos'd to get a Grant to themselves, and set up such another Coinage on their own Account, as soon as this can be set aside: This, *says he*, I believe they will put no-body to the Trouble of proving.

Then he gave me a long Account of the Persons concern'd, the Measures concerted, and the Ad-

Advantages propos'd by thoſe People, who, *as he ſaid*, were thus engag'd againſt Mr. *Wood*'s Patent, and by what Arts they propos'd to bring it before the King, in order to obtain the recalling Mr. *Wood*'s Grant: When I wou'd have ask'd him, by what ſecret Management they had been able to bring it into Parliament, and brought the Houſes to eſpouſe it, as they had done; he took me ſhort, and ſeem'd angry, reminding me, that he had ſaid, he wou'd not meddle with that Part, or ſo much as name the Parliament, in all his Diſcourſe; that he cou'd give me a ſufficient Account of the Matter without it; and that I might enquire that Part of ſome-body elſe, if I found his Relation was imperfect.

I pacify'd him as well as I cou'd, and brought him to go on; then he gave himſelf ſome *looſe* at the Injuſtice and Unfairneſs of this Proceeding; how they abus'd the People, in laying the Complaint in their Names, who, *as he ſaid*, he was well inform'd, never complain'd at all, or had any Inclination to do ſo: Not the Privy-Council, *he ſaid*, not the Lord Lieutenant, not the Mayor and Aldermen of *Dublin*, or of any other City, had ever any Petitions, or Repreſentations, againſt the *Farthings* and *Halfpence*; no Grand-Jury ever preſented them; no Merchants; *in a Word, he added*, that no Man, or Society of Men, open'd their Mouths againſt them; nay, *adds he*, I may ſay, not a Dog wagg'd his Tongue againſt them, 'till this Fire burſt out, as from a ſecret Mine (like a Powder-Plot) to blow up both *Patent* and *Patentee*, in order to ſet up another in its Room.

He

He goes on then to tell me, that this being the ſecret Hiſtory of the Thing itſelf, the Perſons concern'd in it were not ſo ſecret, but that many People gueſs'd at their Names, as well as their Undertaking; and it was given out, that they were Men of ſuch Figure and Intereſt, that they did not doubt they ſhou'd obtain their Requeſt, *namely*, To ſet aſide the *Patent : He ſaid*, it was not known at firſt which way they wou'd go to work, or what Meaſures they wou'd take to get this done, much leſs was it ſo much as gueſs'd, that they wou'd get the Parliament to eſpouſe it: Nor, *adds he*, do I ſay yet, that the Parliament did appear in it, by the procuring of theſe Men, and therefore I ſay nothing to that; for he kept cloſe to the Point, that he wou'd not concern the Parliament in any Part of his Diſcourſe, nor wou'd he ſuffer me ſo much as to name them on that Occaſion.

Thus, *he ſaid*, the firſt Prejudices began in Avarice and private Intereſt, among a Sett of Men, who form'd their Deſign wholly and ſolely upon the View of their own Advantages.

As ſoon as they had form'd their Deſign, *he ſaid*, they ſet their Wheels to Work, to raiſe Complaints among the People, againſt the *Copper-Money*; and tho', *he ſaid*, they went about it with the utmoſt Subtlety and Art, and ſpread their empty Objections among the People, by their Agents, in ſeveral Parts of the Kingdom, yet they cou'd never make any-thing of it, nor bring their Clamours to be popular; for the People be-

being ſenſible of the Utility of the *Copper-Money*, not only by Judgment or Opinion, but by Experience, and by feeling the Difference in their Trade, cou'd never be brought to join with them in their Complaints, much leſs to make any Application to the Government againſt them; tho', *as he ſaid*, he was inform'd, much Endeavour was us'd to bring them to it; ſo that, *in a Word, he ſaid*, they ſeem'd diſcourag'd, and ſilent again; and People began to think, they had given over the Deſign; but in this, *he added*, we were miſtaken; for as Avarice is unwearied, they ſeem'd to imitate the fam'd Reſolution,

——— *Acheronta movebo.*

Then he told me, he heard, that a little before the meeting of the Parliament, they had renew'd their Attack, and try'd ſome great Perſon; he does not ſay (neither was he certain) who it was, but intimates ſome Man of Note; and that finding ſtill no Encouragement (every unprejudic'd Perſon being againſt them) they gave it out, that they wou'd bring it into Parliament; and, *ſays he*, I hear (ſince I came away) it has been brought into Parliament; but that, *adds he*, as alſo being ſince my arriving in *England*, I will have nothing to ſay to.

Here he ſeem'd to ſtop, as if he had done, and ſo indeed he had, as to the Hiſtorical Part of his Account; but I, who wanted much to hear his Opinion of the Arguments on both Sides, ſoon ſet him on again.

But

But pray, *says I*, what had they to ſay againſt the *Farthings* and *Halfpence?* for you ſay they were evidently uſeful to the Country.

I did indeed, *ſays he*, affirm to *thee*, that the People were pleas'd with them, and found them very beneficial; and I own, my Opinion is, they were really ſo; but *thou* know'ſt that greater People than I, ſay they are of another Opinion: Now this he ſaid with a kind of a *Grin*, that in my Thoughts intimated a Contempt of thoſe Opinions; and then he went on, *and told me*, That as to the Arguments thoſe Men brought againſt the Copper-Money, before he came away; they were, *he ſaid*, the weakeſt, and moſt empty, that ever he cou'd have expected to have come from Men of Sence, and that they had no Weight at-all in them; and even the Common People began, *to uſe his own Words*, to have them in Deriſion.

Firſt, *he ſaid*, they gave it out, that they were uſeleſs; that there was no Occaſion for them; that Farthings and Halfpence, indefinitely and merely as Farthings and Halfpence, were of no Service to the Kingdom of *Ireland*; that they were of no Advantage to the Commerce; *nay, he added*, they went farther at length, for they wou'd have it be, that they were prejudicial and deſtructive to Trade; but they ſeem'd to forget in this, that they were preparing a Mine againſt their own Project, and alſo that the common Opinion of the People was againſt them; and indeed, they began to expoſe themſelves

ſelves by it, to ridicule and Laughter; ſeeing *he ſaid*, they dropt that Part, tho' not without acknowledging it to be a Miſtake, and then publickly own'd, that they wou'd have thoſe *English Farthings* and *Halfpence* cry'd down; and that they wou'd ſupply the Country with others coin'd among themſelves; and to make this look a little popular, they talk'd of ſetting to-work upon ſome Copper-Mines, which were formerly diſcover'd in their own Country.

This, *he ſaid*, had been a little more rational, if they cou'd ha' got over two Things, *namely*, (1.) Upon what foot this cou'd be done, if what they had given-out before, and had not yet recall'd, were true; *namely*, That meer *Farthings* and *Halfpence* were deſtructive to the Trade of the Kingdom. (2.) That the Kingdom had no need of them.

But firſt, to blaſt the *Farthings* and *Halfpence* in general, as *deſtructive* and *needleſs*, and then tell the World, they intended to *make ſome themſelves*; this was ſo plain a Diſcovery, *he ſaid*, that whatever it did in *Ireland*, he obſerv'd the People got hold of it here in *England*, and almoſt made a Jeſt of the *Iriſh* Nation, for being ſo groſsly impos'd upon.

Upon this, *he ſaid*, they pull'd in their Horns a little, *as it were*, and taking Breath, they began upon a new Sett of Arguments; but theſe, *he ſaid*, were (in the examining them) found to be as weak, and had as little Weight in them as the other, only that indeed there was not ſo groſs an

Abſurdity, nor ſo barefac'd an Inſult upon the Country, in them, as in the other.

Then he told me, how their Emiſſaries ran up and down, exclaiming againſt the Injuſtice of putting a Coinage upon them from *England*; that it was an Invaſion of the Liberties of the People; that it was a Monopoly, and a Piece of Arbitrary Power; nay, ſome went farther, and reflected upon the Grant itſelf, and conſequently upon the Perſon granting it; and that it was a dangerous Precedent at beſt; that the King had been impos'd upon by *William Wood*, and *his Accomplices*; and had had the State of Affairs in *Ireland* very much miſrepreſented to him, inſinuating, *he ſaid*, that the King had granted this *Patent*, without the Advice of his Council, or without being duly inform'd of the State of Things in *Ireland*.

This was a ſure Card, *he ſaid*, to bring all the Papiſts, and Enemies to the *Government*, into the Party, and to make them univerſally Enemies to the *Copper-Coinage*, they being known to be forward, and glad of an Opportunity to cloſe with any-thing, which they think will make a Clamour at the *Engliſh Government*, or the preſent Adminiſtration under the Reign of King *GEORGE*.

This was a wicked, but a very politick Step, *he ſaid*, for then (and not till then) the Complaint at the *Engliſh Farthings* and *Halfpence* began to be loud, and make a Noiſe; and that Noiſe to be propagated in the remoteſt Parts

of

of the Country; and thus, *added he*, Friend *Wood* suffers in good Company, for the Clamour at the *Farthings* and *Halfpence* became really a Clamour at the *Government*.

Well, *said I*, but why was this so weak and so empty a Complaint?

Why *truly*, *said he*, because it was *not Truth*, and then he went of his own Accord into a Discourse upon the Merits of the *Patent*, and particularly upon the Right the King had to grant such a *Patent*: The Clamour against *England*, *he said*, and particularly against the King, was not only an ill-natur'd thing, but was without sufficient ground; for, *said he*, they can't deny but the Coinage is the King's; that it is his Prerogative, and one of the ordinary Appendixes to the Right of *Government*; that the King (in all Nations where they have Kings reigning) appoint the Coinage of Money; that the Image and Superscription tell whose it is; and that *Ireland*, no more than *England* or *Scotland* cou'd complain against it; in both which Places, as he understood it, *he said*, the Coinage was appointed by the King; and particularly, *Farthings* and *Halfpence* had formerly been coin'd in *England*, for the Account of private Persons, and that by *Patent*, or *Grant*, in the same manner as was now in *Ireland*; and therefore the granting, or appointing, such a Coinage cou'd not be illegal or arbitrary.

Then he took Notice of the Terms of the *Patent* itself; the Care his Majesty had taken of the Rights and Properties of his Subjects of *Ireland*,

land, in the Terms of the Grant, and in the Limitations of the Privileges given to the *Patentee*; and as a Digreſſion, he expreſs'd himſelf very largely, and indeed more fully than I expected from one of his Profeſſion, in Defence of his Majeſty's Conduct, and of the Miniſters of State alſo, in this very Grant.

The King, *he ſaid*, had ſhewn ſuch a Care and Concern, for the Good of all his Subjects in *Ireland*, as well for their Liberties, as the Proſperity of their Trade, in all the Articles of this *Patent*, as evidently ſhew'd, he fully underſtood the true Intereſt of the Kingdom, and the State of his People *there*; and that he neither was, or cou'd be impos'd upon by my Friend *Wood*, or any-one elſe; and ſuch a Care as ought to make 'em aſham'd (whoever they were) who had ſuggeſted to the contrary: *Then he went on, and told me* all the Limitations, which were inſerted in the *Patent*, by which the Fineneſs of the Metal, with the Weight and Value of the *Farthings* and *Halfpence* were aſcertain'd, that ſo the People might not be injur'd in either, the Quantity alſo to be coin'd aſcertain'd, that they might not be glutted with an exorbitant Sum; and that, *after all*, the People were entirely left at Liberty to take *them*, or refuſe *them*, no Man having any Power to impoſe one ſingle *Farthing* or *Halfpenny* upon them, without their Conſent.

Here he expatiated again upon the Difference between the mild and gentle Reign of King *GEORGE*, and the former Tyranny which they

they groan'd under, in the Times of King *Charles* II. and King *James* II. and the falſe Money and Copper-Money impos'd in both theſe Reigns; particularly the laſt, when little more than a Copper *Halfpenny* was made current for *Half a Crown*; but this (however handſomely indeed expreſs'd) I omit for want of Room.

He likewiſe enlarg'd upon the Conduct and Fidelity of the *Britiſh* Miniſters of State, in the ſeveral Inſpections, References, and Reports from one to another, in the ordinary Forms of paſſing this *Patent*; how it had all the mature Conſideration, and Conſultation, as well before the *Privy-Council*, as the *Treaſury*, the *Attorney-General*, and the *Lord-Chancellor*, thro' all whoſe Hands it ſeverally paſs'd; in order that nothing unjuſt, illegal, or arbitrary, or hard, and ſevere to the People of *Ireland*, ſhou'd paſs, or be allow'd in it: Particularly he ſpoke [with the utmoſt Regard] of Mr. *Wa——le*, who, *he ſaid*, fully underſtood the Nature of the Thing, and he was not to be impos'd upon by any-body, in ſuffering ſuch a *Grant* to paſs in the King his Maſter's Name, without ſo many Precautions and Proviſions, as wou'd for ever make it impoſſible for the worſt Enemy the King had, to lay any juſt Reproach, either upon the Nature of the *Grant*, or the Manner of granting it: *And here he told me*, That beſides the Care taken to limit the *Patentee* [as above] from any Miſapplication of the *Patent*, to the Injury or Burden of the Subject, due Care was alſo taken to appoint ſuch a *Checque* and *Comptrole* over the *Patentee*, as that it ſhou'd not be in his Power to make

 any

any Excurſions, beyond the Bounds of the ſaid Powers granted; and to finiſh all, the *Comptoller* [thus appointed] was to make report, from time to time, to the *Lords of the Treaſury*, of all that ſhould be done in Purſuance of the *Patent*: This, *he ſaid*, was particularly owing to the Conduct of Mr. *Wa - - - le*; of whom he ſaid a great-deal, and greatly to his Advantage, which I have not Room to bring in here.

I confeſs, I was ſurpriz'd to hear all this from a Stranger, who had liv'd thus remote; and was extreamly glad, to find his Majeſty, and his Miniſters of State, ſo well treated; and that the King eſpecially, whoſe Actions [I was before aſſur'd] are always guided with the moſt exquiſite Care, and Concern, for the Good of his Subjects, in all his Dominions; I ſay, I was extreamly glad, to find his Majeſty had ſo much Juſtice done him, and that his whole Adminiſtration was ſo effectually vindicated by a plain [but well-meaning] Man, ſo remote from the Place where theſe Things were done.

But I confeſs, when he told me, that by this *Grant* the People of *Ireland* were left ſo entirely free in this whole Affair, that they might take the ſaid Copper-Money, or refuſe it, as they pleas'd; that not the meaneſt Perſon in the Kingdom was to be impos'd upon, or oblig'd to accept them in Payment, or deliver their Goods for them; I ſay, when I heard this, and that he pull'd out a Copy of the *Grant*, and ſhew'd it me in ſo many Words, I was, from that Moment, entirely at a loſs, to find which Way the

In-

Injury to the People of *Ireland* cou'd be made out, or the Damage to their Trade be made rational; but then I pull'd out ſome Printed Papers, which I had met with in the Town, where this Matter was very much canvas'd, as particularly *Miſt's Journal, the Whitehall Evening-Poſt, Boyer's* ſcandalous *Political State*, and ſuch like Pamphlets; and began to enter into ſome Diſcourſe about them.

But he took me ſhort with a Queſtion: Do'ſt *thou* know, *ſaid he*, what our People in *Ireland* ſay of thoſe Libels? No, *ſays I*; Why they ſay, *ſays he*, that Friend *William Wood* the *Patentee*, had hir'd ſome ſubtle Fellow to write a Libel, and publiſh it in *Miſt's Journal, &c.* which was to be perform'd weakly and ſcandalouſly, to form Cavils againſt the Patent, that he might have the Advantage of confuting and expoſing them; as thoſe who write Dialogues make the Enquirer propoſe none but weak Queſtions, that they may be anſwer'd to the Advantage of the Party he writes for.

I told him, that was begging the Queſtion, and alledging nothing, eſpecially as to the Objections about the Value, and the Injury done the People: Nay, *ſays he*, I do not tell *thee* that 'tis ſo, but that indeed it is done very weakly and fooliſhly, that cannot be denied.

But one thing, *he ſaid*, cou'd not be omitted as to theſe Libels; *namely*, How much concern'd the Party who oppos'd this Patent, were, to make their Clamours popular; and that you in *England ſaid he*, ſhou'd hear one ſide of the Queſtion, where you cou'd not ſo readily know what the Sentiments of the People in *Ireland* were, which is the other ſide of it: *Then he obſerv'd*, how unjuſt and unfair the Way of Arguing was; that ſeeing the ſmall Copper-Money is chiefly appointed for the Uſe of the Common People, and that in the Retail Trade, thoſe People are indeed, beſt able to judge whether they had Need of them, and whether they were any Convenience to them or no; yet *in Truth, ſays he*, they have not been enquir'd of in this Matter.

Here he made another Digreſſion upon the Want they had been in for many Years, of ſuch Species of Money; how Retailers, for want of ſmall Money, were oblig'd to keep long Scores, and give long Credit to their Cuſtomers, for little things, till they were frequently forgot, or more frequently loſt; that thoſe who wou'd not keep ſuch Scores, and give ſuch Credit, were oblig'd to ſit ſtill, and not ſell their Goods; ſo that Trade was cramp'd, and made both difficult and hazardous: That all the Help they had againſt this, was from ſeveral ſorts of ſmall Money, ſuch as *Rapps*, *French Threepences*, *Rials*, and ſuch like; which, in the firſt Place, *he ſaid*, did not ſupply the want of *Farthings* and *Halfpence*, their Quantity being ſmall: And, 2. They were brought into *Ireland* much more to the Loſs of the Publick, than the Copper-Money now complain'd of.

For Brevity ſake, I omit a great deal of what he offer'd on that Account, wherein I thought it was ſo evident that *Ireland* was in great Want of of a Copper Coinage, that I wonder'd much at what I had heard here in *England* upon that Subject: But to go on, I then ask'd him what he said to all the Calculations which I shew'd him in our printed Papers, of the great Loss to the Publick, which there wou'd necessarily be in this Money at last, the exorbitant Gain of the *Patentee*, and the Injustice of both.

He told me, It was evident to any that wou'd impartially look into that Matter, that those Calculations were all false and unjust; and that they were made, by Persons who either mistook thro' Ignorance, or from a worse Principle; and that he wou'd undertake to convince me, that not one of them was justly drawn up; *he added*, that he cou'd easily confute them all; nay, *added he*, even *Friend Wood* himself, or those who have written in his Defence, have not given the due Weight to his own Cause; but much more is to be said on that Occasion.

I wou'd have enter'd, one by one, into the general Valuations on the one side, and on the other, which I shew'd him in the printed Papers; but *he said*, it needed not; that he had seen them all, and that he wou'd give me a few Explanations, which if I thought fit to bestow my Thoughts upon, wou'd enable me to give full Answers to them all, wherever I met with them.

First, *he said*, No Man ought to suppose, that a Coinage of *Farthings* and *Halfpence* cou'd be set-up, wherein the Coin shou'd bear the full Weight and Value of the Principles from which

it

it was form'd; or that there ſhou'd not be an Allowance for the preparing the Metal, and the Incidents attending it; for the Coinage itſelf, and the Utenſils, Places of Workmanſhip, Officers, and Perſons employ'd, *that is to ſay*, Labour, *and the like*; the general Coinage *ſays he*, is not done without it.

Secondly, *he ſaid*, No Man ought to ſuppoſe, that the Grant was given to any Perſon for ſuch an Undertaking, attended with ſo much Riſque, Application and Expence, and where ſo great a Stock alſo was requir'd,and that he,*the Undertaker*, ſhou'd not have a reaſonable Gain from it, for the Encouragement of the Undertaking.

Thirdly, *he ſaid*, if theſe Allowances for the Expences, and Incidents in preparing and coining this Money, did not exceed the like Allowances, which have uſually been made in the like Caſes, [except where the different Circumſtance of the Country made it reaſonable]then the *Patentee* has not put any-thing upon the World, which is not juſtifiable by the Cuſtom and Uſage of *Patentees*, in like Caſes, and alſo by the Privileges and Grants of this particular *Patent*.

Theſe three Conſiderations, *he ſaid*, wou'd effectually remove all juſt Complaints from the Perſon, or Conduct, of the *Patentee*; and as to the Value of his *Farthings* and *Halfpence*, and as to the Advantage or Diſadvantage to Trade, and to the Publick by them, he wou'd ſpeak to that Part by itſelf.

As

As to the Value of the Copper, the Expence of Coinage, and Profit of the *Patentee*, he ſtated them together thus :

Firſt, he objected, that there was ſome Debate about the current Value of Copper in *Ireland*, which ſome wou'd have be call'd 1 *s.* *per* Pound, others 1 *s.* 2*d.* *per* Pound ; but as he ſaid, he had been a Merchant, and had imported Copper himſelf, as well from *Sweden* as from *England*, and likewiſe from *Barbary*, he cou'd not afford to ſell the Copper in Bulk, under 14 *d.* but often ſold it for 15 *d.* *per* Pound ; that if Mr. *Wood*, by buying it in *England*, did get it cheaper, that was not the Queſtion here at-all ; but we ought to ſuppoſe it at 1 *s.* 2 *d.* *per* Pound.

Now, *ſays he*, I am not to enquire what the Profit to the *Patentee* immediately is, upon this Pound of Copper, for that is not the Queſtion ; but what it is more than the Profit of the like Coinage in *England*, and then ſee what Reaſons can be given for the Difference ; and by this it will appear whether the *Patentee* is chargable with Exorbitance, or not.

In *England*, *ſays he*, a Pound of Copper makes 45 *Halfpence*, ſometimes 46 ; in *Ireland*, by this new Patent, we have 60 ; ſo that Friend *Wood* ſays, he makes 7 *d.* *halfpenny* in a Pound of *Copper* more of his Coinage than is made in *London*.

I was

I was surpriz'd at his Way of reckoning, for I was going to draw the Account out in Columns, as the printed Papers have done; but he took me short; No, no, *he said*, their Business was not to enquire what Mr. *Wood* got by the Coinage, but what he got more than was gotten by the same Works in *England*; for if they in *Ireland* had but Neighbours Fare, it was what cou'd not be objected against: Therefore, *says he*, I have nothing to do with the Expence of preparing the Metal, or of the Coinage, the Allowances on one hand or other; here is 7 *d. halfpenny per* Pound Difference, let us see how Friend *Wood* accounts for that, and what he has to say why he shou'd make *Ireland* pay 7 *d halfpenny per* Pound more than *England* pays for the same Species.

Well, *said I*, this is a short Way of coming at the Question, indeed; pray go on.

Why first, *says he*, the Copper in *Ireland* is granted to be of the Value of 1 *s.* 2 *d. per* Pound, which is 2 *d.* more than in *England*; so there is 2 *d.* of the 7 *d. halfpenny*; then there is the Difference of Exchange upon his Money, which at 10 *per Cent.* is 3 *d.* in the Half-Crown more; but because a very critical Opposer may insist, that these two Articles relating only to the Difference of Value between *England* and *Ireland*, are therefore in some respect the same, I will set by the Difference of the Price of Copper in this part of the Discourse, and only take the bare Exchange of Money, which the *Patentee* must sink, to to bring back his Money to *England*, in order to go to Market for more Copper.

This Rate of Exchange being one time with another 10 *per Cent.* is 2 *s. per l.* which is juſt 3 *d.* on the Pound of Copper.

Then, *ſays he*, there is the Charge of ſhipping the Coin, ſuppoſe at *Briſtol*, or *London*, when finiſh'd; the Freight to *Ireland*; the Landing there; the Riſque of the Sea; the Charge on-ſhore, *ſuch as* Warehouſe-room, Commiſſion to the Perſons diſpoſing of it, and Commiſſion again for remitting back the Effects: If all this is not to be computed at 10 *per Cent.* more, I muſt ſee ſome Reaſons given to the contrary, which I do not ſee yet, before I allow it.

He then went on to innumerate ſeveral other Particulars, which added to Mr. *Wood*'s Charge, as well before, as after the Coinage here, which the Coinage at the *Tower* is not loaded with; Particularly, that all Mr. *Wood*'s Servants, and Workmen, Engines, Tools, Buildings, and Conveniences, are hir'd on purpoſe, and maintain'd ſolely for this one Work; and conſequently his Charge of Servants and Workmen is greater, than at the *Tower*, where all things are prepar'd for other Branches of the Coinage, as well as that of the Copper-Money, and where the Servants are employ'd in common upon the one as well as the other, and conſequently the Charge is not equal: But all this, *he ſaid*, he only mention'd, for that beſides this, the other two Articles had brought his Calculation beyond what his Argument

ment call'd for; and it appear'd, that *Ireland* had their *Farthings* of Mr. *Wood* cheaper, the Circumstances of their Situation consider'd, one *Halfpenny* in a Pound-weight, than *England* receiv'd theirs from the *Tower.*

With this Addition also, That if the *Farthings* and *Halfpence*, both in *England* and *Ireland*, were all to be melted down, and reduc'd into meer Copper-Metal, the said Copper wou'd sell for 2 *d. per* Pound weight more than the reduc'd Copper in *England* wou'd sell for; so that *Ireland* wou'd be less a Loser than *England*, by 1 *s.* 4 *d. per l.* Sterling; which is 6 *l.* 13. 4 *per Cent.*

I told him, I cou'd not deny but his Calculation was just so far.

Well then, *said he*, I have gain'd that Point, and *thou* must allow, that Friend *Wood* does not get more by the *Farthings* and *Halfpence* in *Ireland*, than the Government gains, (if it be gain'd) by the like Species coin'd at the *Tower.*

Likewise, *said he*, *thou* can'st not but see, that the *Government* of *England* has acted not only with a due Regard to Justice, but with a prudent Regard to the Subjects of *Ireland*; not to lay any Burthen upon them, but what the Nature of the thing, and the Circumstances of the Kingdom made necessary; and that they are so far from having reason to complain of being oppress'd, or impos'd arbitrarily upon, and having harder Terms than *England*, that on the contrary, they have rather the Advantage, than the Disadvantage,

tage, of *England*, in this Grant, and that in every Part of it.

But where then, *said I*, is Mr. *Wood*'s Profit? *I tell thee*, says he, *speaking a little warm*, That's nothing to me, or to *thee*, as to the Matter in debate: If there is a Profit in the Coinage in the *Tower*, so there may be to him in his Coinage at *Bristol*; and yet even in that, as I have told *thee* already, his Profit must be much less than theirs at the *Tower*, many Ways; but that, *he said*, was one of the present Questions which he challeng'd me to answer, if I cou'd, *namely*, Whether Mr. *Wood*, Friend *Wood he call'd him*, had made any Advantage, by virtue of this Grant, more than was made of the like Coinage in *England?* And whether *Ireland* had not their *Farthings* and *Halfpence* as cheap, *their own Circumstances only excepted*, as *England* had theirs? Which indeed, I cou'd not deny.

But I have not done with *thee* yet, *says my* QUAKER; for I shall now undertake to tell *thee*, and perhaps prove it as plainly as I have done the other:

1. That as the *Patentee* really does, and indeed must, dispose of these *Farthings* and *Halfpence*, they are in effect, very little Loss to *Ireland*; no, tho' they were to be reduc'd immediately to their first Principles, and sold in Bulk as meer Copper.
2. That as he may dispose of them, and as I, *says the* QUAKER, am told, he has offer'd to dispose of them, they will be so far from

from being any Loſs to the publick Stock of the Kingdom, that if *Ireland* will do Juſtice to the *Patentee* and his Aſſigns, they ſhall after a certain Period of Years, call them all in at Demand, and he ſhall pay for them the full Value they were at firſt iſſu'd out at, and that in the current Money of *Ireland*.

I look'd a little ſurpriz'd at him, and deſir'd to know how this cou'd be made out? *He told me*, it wou'd be too long to enter upon at that time, unleſs I had a great-deal more Patience than he thought I had; however, as he found me eager to be inform'd, and that, *he ſaid*, I might ſet it in a clear Light to others, *he told me*, he wou'd enter a little upon the Firſt, and if we had not Time for the reſt, it ſhou'd be adjourn'd to our next Leiſure.

He began then with the Firſt, *viz*.

He bid me obſerve, that as *Farthings* and *Halfpence* were the loweſt Species of Coin, ſo they were diſpos'd of, *generally ſpeaking*, among the meaneſt ſort of the trading People; and in Conſequence of this, *he ſaid*, they were ordinarily exchang'd for the meaneſt Species of Money; and that particularly, for *French Threepences* and *Groats*, quarters of *Livres*, *and the like*, and at the beſt, for *Rials* or *Cobbs* by weight, or *Engliſh* Money by tale.

Of the laſt we cou'd not ſuppoſe, *he ſaid*, much was receiv'd; but of the former, the greateſt Part; it ought then to be enquir'd, *he*

ſaid,

said, what Loss there wou'd be to the Kingdom of *Ireland* upon that *French* and Foreign Money, those *Threepences*, *Quarter-pieces*, &c. in case they were to be reduc'd to Metal? and whatever that was, so much ought to be deducted out of the Loss which it might be suppos'd *Ireland* wou'd lose by the Reduction of *Farthings* and *Halfpence* into Copper; for (*to make it plainer*) *he said*, If *Ireland* buys the *Farthings*, &c. when they are current, or to make them current, tho' they are not of the full Value for which they are made current, and pays for them in another Coin, which is likewise not of the full Value for which it passes as current, then no more of the Loss by the Deficiency cou'd be plac'd to the Account of the *Farthings* and *Halfpence*, than the Difference was between the Loss on the separate Reduction in the several Species: *For Example*, he said,

Suppose the *French* Threepences, *&c.* pass in *Ireland* for Threepence, and being reduc'd, are found not to be of more Value than Twopence, losing thereby one Third, when they are turn'd into Metal, and sold in Bulk.

And supposing, *tho' not granting*, that the Farthings lost one Half, when reduc'd into Metal; why then, *he added*, *Ireland* cou'd be said to lose no more by the *Farthings*, than the Difference between one Third and one Half, which wou'd be thus,

Suppose { 10 French *Threepence cost at current Price* 2.6.
{ 1 *Pound Copper Farthings cost* —— 2.6.

When reduc'd { the *1st sell for* 1 s. 8d. *Loss* 10d.
{ the *2d sell for* 1 s. 3d. *Loss* 15d.

So that here is but 5*d.* by 2*s.* 6*d.* Loſs to *Ireland*, more than *Ireland* was in a declar'd State of loſing before; which, *ſaid he*, is but $\frac{1}{6}$ Part, and this not till the Money is reduc'd neither: Let them ſhew me, *ſaid he*, any Copper Coinage made current in the World on ſo eaſy Terms: Then he ſhew'd me how the ſame ſtood in *England*; there, *ſaid he*, 45 *Halfpence* are made of a Pound of Copper, and paſs for 1 *s.* 10 *d. ob.* and are bought for ſo much in good Standard Silver or Gold; when theſe are reduc'd to Metal, *ſaid he*, they ſell but for 1 *s.* and ſo loſe 10*d. ob. per* Pound, which is above double the Loſs of that in *Ireland*.

But, *ſaid I*, if they ſell the *Farthings*, *&c.* in *Ireland*, for *French* Threepences, they likewiſe put off thoſe Threepences again in *Ireland*, and ſo the Publick bears the Loſs of both.

This, *he ſaid*, was dancing in a Circle; for ſo the *Farthings* might buy *Threepences*, and the *Threepences* buy *Farthings*, to the end of the Chapter; which neither made one way or other, the Subſtance being the ſame, and the Species the ſame alſo; but the Loſs was not till the End.

But then I objected, that he plac'd the Reduction at 15 *d. per* Pound on Copper, which was at beſt, but at 14 *d.* *He anſwer'd*, That was ſtated to make good the Example, and not to determine the Value; but that the Caſe was ſtill equal; for that neither were thoſe *Threepences* worth 2 *d.* each; and if I inſiſted upon that, he might put the Caſe upon the *Rapps*, another ſcandalous Foreign Coin, which went current in *Ireland*; and upon

upon the *Scots Bodles*, and *Baubees*, both which went current in *Ulster*, and were, tho' *Copper*, considerably lighter, and leſs worth, than the *New Farthings* and *Halfpence* coin'd by Friend *William Wood*, as he call'd him.

I cou'd not deny the Force of this Argument, nor cou'd I avoid the Conſequence of it; which he laid down thus:

If then, *ſaid he*, this *New Copper-Coin* be purchas'd with another *Coin* equally deficient, which yet is current in the ſame Kingdom of *Ireland*; then *Ireland* can loſe nothing by the *Farthings* and *Halfpence*; becauſe 'tis evident, they wou'd only ſupply the Place of Foreign Coins, and prevent the Encreaſe, which are already receiv'd at a like Loſs, and which if the *Copper Money* did not come in, would daily encreaſe, the Want of ſmall Money appearing to grow greater and greater in *Ireland*.

Having gone through this Part of his Argument, which he enlarg'd much more upon, than I have room here to give an Account of, I preſs'd him to enter upon his Second Article, which, *he ſaid*, was ſo ſignificant, and which I ſeem'd to wonder ſo much at; and I promis'd him my Attention, being, *as indeed I was*, impatient to hear his Explanation of what I thought was ſo myſterious: So he repeated the whole Article; for I am not afraid, *ſaid he*, or doubtful that I ſhall not make it out to *thy* Satisfaction: The Article is as follows, *viz.*

First, *he ſaid*, he laid it as a Foundation, that *Friend Wood, ſo he call'd the Patentee*, ſhou'd ſell his *Farthings* and *Halfpence* for Manufactures ei-ther of Wool or Flax, as he told me he had offer'd to do for ſome Part of them.

I reply'd, I knew that Mr. *Wood* intended to do ſo, and that if he did not immediately exchange the the *Farthings* and *Halfpence* for Linnen and Wool-len Manufactures, he was ſuch a Friend to the Commerce of *Ireland*, and had reſolv'd to encou-rage it ſo much, that he reſolv'd to veſt a great Part of the Species he receiv'd for them in thoſe Goods, and to Ship the ſame for the *Weſt-Indies*.

Very well, *he ſaid*; then he undertook to prove that for all thoſe *Farthings* and *Halfpence* which ſhould be ſo veſted in Woollen or Linnen Manu-factures of *Ireland*, to be carry'd out of the King-dom, whether to *England*, or the *Weſt-Indies*, *Ireland* ſhou'd gain conſiderably, tho' the ſaid *Farthings* and *Halfpence* were immediately melted again, and reduc'd into *Copper* Metal.

I liſten'd earneſtly to this Diſcourſe, and waited the Demonſtration; which he began thus:

Previous, *ſaid he*, to the Computations and Schemes that may be neceſſary to explain this Article, *thou* muſt grant me one juſt Diſtinction; *namely*, That we are not now ſpeaking of the Profit or Loſs accruing to to this or that private Perſon in *Ireland*, in any Part of what may be ſpoken of about the

the *Farthings* and *Halfpence*, but of the Profit or Loſs to the publick Stock of *Ireland* as a Nation.

For Example, Firſt, *he ſaid*, the Value of any Product form'd by the Induſtry of the People, was of no real Advantage to, and did not encreaſe the publick Stock of the Country, if that Product was not ſent away, and exported out of the Kingdom; for as to what was conſum'd at-home, whatever was gain'd by the ſeveral Artificers and Manufacturers thro' whoſe Hands it paſs'd, was loſt again in his Hands who was the laſt Conſumer, and ſo the general Stock remain'd the ſame.

2. Of thoſe Manufactures which are exported, no Part can be eſteem'd a Diminution of the publick Stock, but the firſt Principles of the Manufacture, all the reſt is Gain to the Stock; and conſequently whatever is return'd, or paid for it, is clear Profit to the publick Stock of the Country.

Now, *ſays he*, for Example, if a Pound of Wool, coſting 3 *d.* by various Improvements, arrives to the Value of 5 *s.* in Manufactures (as it is manifeſt in ſome Manufactures, it will double that Value,) and if then *thy Friend Wood* gives two Pound of *Copper Halfpence*, value 5 *s.* for this Pound of Wool manufactur'd, tho' this two Pound of *Halfpence* be immediately melted, and reduc'd into *Copper* Metal, and ſold for 14 *d. per* Pound, which is 2 *s.* 4 *d.* the publick Stock of the Kingdom of *Ireland* gains two Shillings and one Penny by the Exchange.

 I con-

I confeſs I was confounded at this Computation, and at firſt did not readily apprehend it, wherefore *I ask'd* him, what came of the almoſt numberleſs Families of Handicrafts, Labourers, and Manufacturers employ'd in bringing the Manufacture ſo wrought from the Fleece to the Merchandize.

Become of them? *ſaid he*, they are all paid by one-another; what they earn, they ſpend; it circulates from one to another; they gain by Work, they eat, and loſe it again, and ſtill 'tis within ourſelves; the publick Stock neither encreaſes or decreaſes by that; but the *Copper* which *thy* Friend brings in, leaves 2 *s.* 1 *d.* of ſolid unconſumable Metal in Specie in the Kingdom, more than the 3 *d.* which it carried away.

This 2 *s.* 1 *d.* is a real Value, it will go to *Scotland*, or *England*, or *Portugal*, or any-where, and exchange itſelf into Gold or Silver, if you pleaſe, and come home as valuable as it went out, and will never dimininiſh, unleſs loſt by ſome ſubſequent Conduct, to which this has no relation.

I had not one Word to ſay againſt this, nor can I ſince, tho' I have propos'd it to ſeveral in the very ſame terms which the QUAKER ſtated it to me; *I ſay*, I cannot meet with one ſubſtantial Objection againſt it, ſo I leave it for any-one to confute, who think they can confute it.

But

But now FRIEND, *says my* QUAKER, I have not done with *thee* yet; my next Queſtion is, If the Profit to the publick Stock be thus great, under the unneceſſary Suppoſition of a Reduction of the *Copper Coin* to its meer firſt Principles, what an immenſe Gain to the publick Stock of *Ireland* muſt it be, if this Coin remains current; for tho' it is true, ſimply conſider'd, that it is of no more Value than the 2 *s.* 1 *d.* to which it may be reduc'd, yet it is really a Loan to the Kingdom of *Ireland* of 2 *s.* 11 *d.* more, in every 5 *s.* current Caſh, which Loan it ſupplies the Nation with, for the Convenience of its Commerce, without any Intereſt; and if there ſhou'd be the Value of 200,000 *l.* in Farthings thus made current for any Number of Years, the Advantage of this in Trade is ſcarce to be computed, ſeeing it is capable (always ſuggeſting it to be laid-out in Manufactures) of keeping the Poor of the whole Kingdom employ'd, and conſuming the Product in a foreign Nation.

And this is the Foundation, *added he*, on which, *I ſaid before, and ſay it now*, let *Ireland* pay Intereſt for this Loan, to the *Patentee*, but at 3 *per Cent.* the *Patentee* may oblige himſelf, his Executors, Adminiſtrators, and Aſſigns, at any time after thirty Years, to call theſe *Farthings* and *Halfpence* all in, and pay for them at the full Rate as *Farthings* and *Halfpence*; or let them be melted down in *Ireland*, and Pay the Difference.

I liſten'd to this Part too, with Attention, tho' it ſeem'd to be but a Speculation; but upon examining it, I cou'd not deny the Fact, or find any Falacy in the reaſoning Part.

My QUAKER ſeeing me ſilent, began to ſmile at me; and now my Friend, *ſaid he*, what Occaſion has here been for ſuch a plentiful Shower of Railery at King *George*, and his Government in *England*? or at the Miniſters of State? or at *Friend Wood? Thou* ſeeſt the World is impos'd upon in the Matter.

Really, *ſays I, thou* haſt made it ſo plain to me, I think they have been impos'd upon indeed; 'tis true, I thought ſo before, but I cou'd not make it out ſo clearly as I can now.

Well, *ſaid he*, I am glad thou art convinc'd at laſt; but now ſhall I ask *thee* a Queſtion or two about what I hear ſince I came to *England?* for *thou*, *ſays he*, may'ſt perhaps, know more of that Part than I do, or, *at leaſt*, *thou* can'ſt, as a Piece of News, tell me whether it be true or not.

What are your Queſtions, *ſays I?*

Why, *ſays he*, one of my Queſtions is this: I underſtand it has been deſir'd of our King, by ſome People, that he ſhou'd iſſue out his Proclamation to forbid the taking theſe *Farthings* and *Halfpence* in the Kingdom of *Ireland*.

I interrupted him there, *and told him*, I believ'd that was his Miſtake, and that, as I was inform'd, inform'd, it was only an Application or Addreſs to the King, to command his Officers and Receivers of the Revenue, not to take them in Payment.

Why, *ſays he*, even what *thou* ſay'ſt, is the ſame thing in a leſſer Degree, but I do not mean that; but as I ſaid to *thee*, I have been inform'd, that ſome People have endeavour'd, or reſolv'd to endeavour, to obtain a Proclamation to command the People not to take them; or, *added he*, to ſpeak in *thy* Country Way in the like Caſes, *to cry them down.*

Well, *ſays I*, and what do you infer from that?

Why, *ſaid he*, I wou'd ask *thee* a Queſtion upon that Subject: Whether wou'd it not be as arbitrary and illegal to have commanded us not to have paſs'd them as current, and not to take them in Payment as current Money, as it wou'd have been to have commanded them to paſs current by virtue of the King's Prerogative?

I anſwer'd, If the Coinage was the King's by Right, and by Prerogative, as he had granted, it cou'd not have been arbitrary either *to cry them up*, or *cry them down*; but both had been in the King's Power to do, without any Complaint juſtly lying againſt it.

He ſaid, I did not keep to the *Terms* of his *Queſtion*; he did not queſtion the Prerogative of the King, *one way or other*; it was none of his Buſineſs or Intention ſo much as to meddle with it; but his

his Queſtion was, Whether one was not as much an act of Tyranny, or Arbitrary Power, as the other?

I told him, Yes, without Queſtion they were equally arbitrary, or equally rightful.

Well then, *ſays he*, with what Aſſurance muſt thoſe Men act, who cou'd firſt cenſure the *Patent* as an illegal Grant, and an arbitrary putting the *Copper Coin* upon the People, tho' it was not impos'd upon them neither, and yet cou'd deſire the King to impoſe the Negative upon them; for it muſt be, that as the *Patent* leaving the People free, they had certainly a Right to refuſe them, as well as to take them; ſo certainly they are ſtill free, and have a Right to take them, as well as refuſe them.

Beſides, *he added*, that he thought we went all upon a wrong Argument here in another Caſe, for want of diſtinguiſhing rightly of the thing; for, *ſays he*, the Grant to *thy* Friend *Wood* does not exert the Prerogative of the King, as is uſual in all Grants, and Patents of this Kind, and that relate to the Coin.

Then he told me, That, *as he had ſaid before*, there had been ſeveral Grants of this Kind before this; and the King of *Great-Britain* had given the *Copper* Coinage to particular Perſons before now, by *Patent*, and that in *England* in particular; nor was it ever eſteem'd to be arbitrary and illegal to declare them current.

But

But that in this Grant the King having with an unuſual Tenderneſs to his People, left it in their Choice, whether to take them, or refuſe them, they were to be therefore diſtinguiſh'd from the general Coinage of the King's Dominions, and were rather a Merchandize than a Coin; and if ſo, *ſays he*, I do not ſee upon what Foundation thoſe Men cou'd proceed, who intended to move the King (if any did do ſo) to *cry them down by Proclamation*, ſeeing, *ſays he*, every Man is free, and it is the undoubted Property of the People, if they have any Property at-all, to deal in, buy and ſell any Goods and Merchandize whatſoever, if not prohibited, and made contraband by Law.

Theſe *Farthings* and *Halfpence* then, *he ſaid*, are nothing but a certain Quantity of *Copper* Metal ſold in ſmall Pieces, and which the King has given Leave to the Proprietor of them to ſtamp with a certain Mark, by which they may be particularly known, and the Value of them aſcertain'd; we are not bound ſo much, *added he*, as to know them by their Names, but they are carried to Market as coin'd *Copper* Metal, and if any will buy them, as no doubt they have a Right to do, *well and good*; then *Wm. Wood*, *thy* Friend, who is the Proprietor, ſells them, as he and the People can agree; if they will not buy, he muſt keep them till they will buy, or otherwiſe diſpoſe of them as he thinks fit.

And juſt thus, *ſays he*, it is in this very Country of *England*, for I need not carry *thee* out of

thy

thy Knowledge for an Example; and then he brought a moſt clever compleat Parallel from the Block-Tin in *Cornwall*: The Tin in *Cornwall, he ſaid*, was as much *a Coin* as my Friend *Wood*'s *Farthings* and *Halfpence* in *Ireland*, and my Friend *Wood*'s *Farthings* and *Halfpence* as much a Merchandize as the Blocks of Tin in *Cornwall*; they are both, *ſays he*, the Property of private Perſons, yet both are ſtamp'd with the ſeveral Marks and Inſcriptions, which are ſeverally appointed by the King's Authority; the Standard of both their Weight and Fineneſs, *adds he*, are likewiſe adjuſted and ſettled by the ſame Authority, and the Works are equally call'd by the ſame Name, *viz.* a Coinage.

The Blocks of Tin are brought to the ſeveral *Stanuary Towns* in *Cornwall* appointed for the Coinage of Tin, and there by the King's Officers they are eſſay'd and coin'd; nor, *adds he*, do I put the Word *Coin'd* upon them, but 'tis call'd ſo there upon the Spot; and when they are thus coin'd, the Goodneſs and Fineneſs of the Metal being firſt aſcertain'd, and then the Blocks are current, *that is*, they are carried to Market, and any-body may buy them that pleaſe.

Thus, *he told me*, it was with Mr. *Wood*'s Coinage; *thy* Friend *Wood*, *ſays he*, does no more, his *Copper* is brought to *Briſtol*, which is his *Stanuary Town*, or Place of Coinage, there they are form'd into ſuch Pieces as the Market calls for, and there the Metal is eſſay'd, and the Value of it aſcertain'd by proper Perſons; then it it is ſtamp'd, and ſuch Marks and Inſcriptions made upon them as is directed by the King's Authority; *and what then?* why then 'tis a current Merchandize, and 'tis carry'd to *Ireland* to Market, where any-body may buy them that pleaſe.

This Conſideration, *he ſaid*, gave the People a Right to buy them, and as *Copper*, in whatever Shape, was not prohibited in *Ireland*, none cou'd be forbid admitting them to be imported, unleſs they were ſo prohibited by Law, or be forbidden to buy them and ſell them, when they were imported, and that when, and as often, and at what Price or Value the Buyer and Seller cou'd agree for.

And by the ſame Rule, *ſays he*, theſe, or any other Goods of the like Nature, may be made current by the common Conſent of the People in any other Part of the King's Dominions; and here he enter'd into a very fine and ingenious Diſcourſe upon the great Eaſe with which a coin'd Merchandize might (the King conſenting) be made current in all the diſtant Parts of the King's Dominions, with due Calculations and Allowances for the intrinſick Value of the Materials, and for the Proportions to the Rates of Exchange, or the Loſs and Gain in the intercourſe of Commerce between *England* and all the ſaid diſtant Places reſpectively.

But when I was big with Expectations for his enlarging on ſo *agreeable* and ſo *improving* a *Subject*, he turn'd it back again to *Ireland*, and the Subject we were

were upon before, in this pleaſant and uſeful manner ; I am not going, *ſays he*, to carry *thee* off of *thy* Argument, to follow my Notions, which perhaps are out of *thy* way, I bring it back to the Caſe in hand, *ſays he*, and to the Proportions in this Coinage of *thy* Friend *Wood* in *Ireland*, and it wou'd not be amiſs, *ſaid he*, to enlarge a little upon the Argument, how well the Value is proportion'd and calculated to the Rate of Exchange, either to *England*, or between *Ireland* and any other Country in *Europe*.

It may not, *ſaid I*, be ſo much out of my way as you imagine, to talk of proportioning a petty Coinage for other Places beſides *Ireland* ; on the contrary, *ſaid I*, I ſhall be very glad to hear you talk on that Subject too, becauſe I fancy you have ſpent ſome Thoughts that way.

Yes, *he ſaid*, he had, but it was too conſiderable a Subject to enter into at preſent, and he wou'd give me an Hour or two by itſelf on that Part, when I wou'd ; but, *he ſaid*, he cou'd not give up this Caſe of the *Copper* Money in *Ireland*, without obſerving one thing more, *viz.* that the Proportions between the current and the intrinſick Value were ſo well calculated and adjuſted, that notwithſtanding all that had been objected in Publick and in Private, yet there was a nearer Proportion in the *Copper* Money, than in any other Foreign Species of Money that were current at that time in the Kingdom ; I mean a Proportion, *ſays he*, to the Value of Exchanges from other Countries ; and that a Foreign Bill of Exchange made Payable at *Dublin*, wou'd much bette better be Paid in *Copper Farthings*, than in *French* or *Dutch*, or any other Money, except only in *English* Guineas; and, *he added*, that there was a greater Weight of Argument lay upon this Part, than I was yet aware of; but this alſo we agreed to adjourn.

He then concluded with telling me, he hop'd he might ſay, that the King and the Miniſters of of State in *England* know the State of Affairs in *Ireland* ſo well, and were ſo heartily concern'd for the publick Good of the Kingdom, that he was in great Hopes they ſhou'd not be depriv'd of the Advantage of this ſmall Coinage, which *ſays he*, if we ſhou'd, it wou'd be an infinite Diſadvantage to our Commerce.

We had a great-deal of Diſcourſe more of this Kind, but I have not room to give any farther Account of it at this Time.

FINIS.

SOME REASONS

Bibliographical note:

this facsimile has been made from a copy in the Beinecke Library of Yale University (NZ.Z724sd)

SOME

REASONS

Shewing the Necessity the People of *Ireland* are under, for continuing to refuse Mr. *Wood*'s Coinage.

By the Author of the Considerations.

Isthuc est Sapere, non quod ante pedes modo est
Videre, sed etiam illa, quæ futura sunt,
Prospicere.——— Teren.

Nullæ sunt occultiores insidiæ, quam quæ latent in simulatione officii, aut in aliquo necessitudinis nomine, nam eum qui palam est adversarius, facile, cavendo vitare possis: hoc vero occultum intestinum ac domesticum malum, non modo existit, verum etiam opprimit, antequam prospicere atque explorare potueris. Cic.

Dublin: Printed in the Year, MDCCXXIV.

To the Right Honourable *Allan*, Lord Viscount *Middleton*, Lord High Chancellor of *Ireland*.

My Lord,

IT *has been constantly observed of your Lordship, that you have found out the Secret, of making the* PATRIOT *and* MINISTER *agree in the same Person; for as you have ever been Remarkable for your Adherence to the Interest of the Crown, so you have always consulted the good of the* Common Wealth. *It is for this Reason, that I presume, to put the following Sheets under your Protection; that my Readers, by seeing your Lordship's Name at the head of them, may be, at the first View, assur'd, they are writ with a just regard to the Prerogative of the King, and the Interest of this Country. I am with the most profound Respect.*

My Lord,

Your Lordships most

Humble and most Obedient

Servant,

D. B.

SOME

REASONS, &c.

WHEN *distinct Property* was settled by the Law of Man, and Traffick became the Business of the whole World, it was absolutely necessary, that some common Measure shou'd be established for the more ready setting a value on the Possessions of Men, and the Goods or Commodities they traded in.

And as it was necessary that this *Common Measure* shou'd always preserve an *Intrinsick Value*, it seems the Reason, that universal Consent fixed on *Gold* and *Silver*, as the properest Materials to constitute such a *Common Measure*. For they being of all other Metals the Purest, and most Durable, and therefore the most proper for Preservation, are, at the same time, the rarest and the most difficult to be come at, which must always continue an *Intrinsick Value* in them.

But However this Value came first to be given *Gold* and *Silver*, we find they were made the *Standard*, or *common Measure of Value*, of all other Commodities; and those two Metals were divided into small Parcels, for the Readier carriage from Place to Place, and in order to Certify the fineness and weight of those pieces, there were Stamps put on them by Publick Authority: and those Pieces, thus stamp'd, were call'd *Money*, which received particular Names, and Denominations, in the different Countries where they were thus stamped or coined.

Yet, taking it as the *Measure of Trade in General*, *Money* does not acquire any *Intrinsick* Value from the Stamp. For be the Material *Gold* or *Silver*, it has no other *Real Value* than in Proportion to its Weight and Fineness; and *Money* may be said to be bought by, and sold for other Commodities, as well as other Commodities are said to be bought by, and sold for *Money*. The

The same may be said of the different Species of *Money*, when compared together : For as *Gold* and *Silver* do reciprocally Measure one another, so the raising the Denomination of the Coin made of either of these Metals, may indeed, give it a greater *Imaginary Estimation* in the Country where it is thus enhaunced, but it can by no Means encrease its *Real Value* in the *Trading World*.

This is plainly proved by daily Experience; and it is certain, that if *Money* made of *Gold*, be in one Country of greater Proportional Value to the Money made of *Silver*, than it is in other Countries; a greater Quantity of *Gold* will be poured into the *Current Cash* of the Nation; but instead thereof, the *Silver* Coin will be drained away. And the same may be said of *Silver Money*, when it exceeds the Price of *Gold*.

That in Fact it is thus, I may refer my Reader to a Consideration of the Present State of the Cash of *Ireland*, and he will find, that ever since the Reduction of Guineas in *Great-Britain*, from Twenty one Shillings and Six Pence, to 21 Shillings, we have been gradually loosing our *Silver* Coin, until at Length we are almost deprived of our *Silver* Species; and this proceeds from the *disproportioned Value* of the *Silver* and *Gold* Coins of *Ireland*, compared with those of *Great-Britain*.

For 100 Pound of *Silver Money* in *England*, is equal to 108 *l.* 6 *s.* 8 *d.* in *Ireland*, and 100 Pound of *Gold* in *England* produces 109 *l.* 10 *s.* 6 *d.* in *Ireland*, so that the *disproportioned Value* of the *Gold Coin* in *Ireland*, to the *Silver Coin*, is 1 *l.* 3 *s.* 10 *d.* on an 100 Pound *English*, which is a Difference great enough to have the Effects we see on the Current Cash of the Nation; and this Consideration alone, will make it plain to every Capacity, how necessary it is that there should always be an Equality of Value, preserved between the different Sorts of Coin that constitute the Current Cash of every Nation.

That this Disproportion between the value of Gold and Silver is Obstructive of Trade, is evident from Experience; and I believe it will readily be allowed, that the Consequences wou'd prove yet more Fatal, if the Disproportion be created between the Coins of those Metals, and *Tokens* made of *Copper*, or any other Metal of inferior Value: And this Mischief will be increased in proportion to the Difference, between

between the *Imaginary* and *Real Value* of the Coins, compar'd with thoſe of other Countries.

For let us give what Name we will to our Coin, and let us raiſe it to ever ſo high an Imaginary Eſtimation, it is moſt certain the real Value of it, is not, by that Means, encreaſed; but that it will always be conſider'd by other Nations, only according to the fineneſs and quantity of the Metal it is compoſed of: So that a Nation that is unhappily led into ſuch Miſtakes, is greatly deceiv'd, and Foreigners have thereby an unavoidable Opportunity given them of drawing away its Riches, by their ſuperior Skill in matters of this Nature.

It has already been ſaid, that *Gold* and *Silver* are the Metals, of which *Money* is made to ſerve as *a general Meaſure of Trade*; and they are the only Metals that have that univerſal Eſteem ſet on them. Yet it was found neceſſary in all Countries, to have Coins made of baſer Metals, in order to ſerve for ſmall Payments: But thoſe Coins never obtained the Credit of being eſteemed among the *Common Meaſures* of Trade.

It is true, that in ſome Countries, the currency of their *Copper Money*, is enforced in a certain Proportion of Payments; but in *England*, and *Ireland*, Tokens made of *Copper*, were never accounted lawful Money, yet for conveniency they are allowed to have a Currency.

It ſeems therefore neceſſary, (ſince ſo baſe a Coin, may by any Means obtain a Currency,) That the Coinage of *Copper-Money* ſhou'd be performed by Publick Authority, and with the ſame Cautions of the *Silver* and *Gold* Coinage. And it is a Matter moſt proper to be taken into the Care of Sovereigns, whoſe Intereſt it is, never for any private Advantage to overſtock their Countries with this ſort of Coin, which is made of a Metal not univerſally accepted, as the Meaſure of Trade.

Upon the whole Matter, the care of the Coin of every Nation, is abſolutely neceſſary, in order to avoid being over-reach'd by other Countries in the courſe of Trade, and alſo to ſet a juſt value on *diſtinct Properties*.

It ought not therefore to be admired, that we are *under great Apprehenſions from the Importing and Uttering Copper Halfpence and Farthings in Ireland, by vertue of the Patent granted to Mr. Wood.* For if it takes effect, the Copper Money of *Ireland* will bear too great a Proportion to the

lawful

lawful Money of the Kingdom; and (tho' the Terms of the Patent shou'd be strictly complied with) wou'd have an imaginary Estimation, so much above the real Value of the Metal; that it wou'd of Necessity *prove highly Prejudicial to his Majesty's Revenue, Destructive of the Trade and Commerce of the Kingdom, and of dangerous Consequence to the Properties of the Subject*; which I hope to prove undeniably, by what I shall say on this Occasion.

To shew *that the Copper Money made by Vertue of this Patent, hath not a just Proportion of Intrinsick Value*: It is only necessary to Observe, that by the Patent, every Pound of Copper is allow'd to be coin'd into 30 Pence; and this is the *Imaginary Value* that is set on this quantity of Copper when made into Half-pence and Farthings. Now the *real Value* of the Metal, (supposing it to be of the finness, requir'd by the Patent) is at most only 12 Pence, and this is the *Intrinsick Value* of 30 Pence, in Tale, of this Coin. So that the Difference between the *Real*, and *Imaginary Value*. of this *Copper Money* is, as 2 to 5, or 60 *l.* loss in 100 l.

But perhaps it will be objected, that *Copper Money* is in all Countries of less Worth than the Denomination that is given to it; and that therefore it is unfair to make an exact Scrutiny into the Difference between the *Imaginary Value* set on such Species of Money, and the *Real Value* of the Material. The first we allow, but at the same time affirm, that there is no trading Nation in the World, that wou'd not be considerably affected in its Trade, if there shou'd be a greater quantity of *Copper Money*, of less intrinsick Value than the Species of *Gold* and *Silver*, thrown into the current Cash of the Nation, than what is absolutly Necessary for small Payments. And if the Power of uttering such base Coin be unconfined, it may in the End utterly ruin the Trade of the most flourishing Country in the World.

For this Reason, in all Countries, the Copper Coinage is under, or shou'd be under, the imediate Direction of the State, for when that Care is taken, it cannot be suppos'd, that any greater quantity of such base Coin will be poured into the current Cash (which is the great Evil to be apprehended) than what is absolutely necessary, for managing the Business of the Nation; and this the Exigency of the People, gives a Demand for, and a natural Currency to. So that when there is only such a quantity of Half-pence and

Farthings

Farthings Current, as are accepted in Payments for the Conveniency of Trade, People receive them without making a nice Enquiry into their intrinsick Value; especially when every one hath a sufficient Security, that he shall not loose by them; because, that as the Prince takes the Benefit of the Coinage to himself, so, it is but reasonable to expect, he must accept the same Coin in Payments to be made into the Exchequer.

Whereas, in the Case of this Patent, the Matter is otherwise: For as the Power of the Coinage is granted to a private Person, we must apprehend he'll have only his own Interest in View, and that he will always pursue it, tho' at the Expence of the Publick. He will therefore supply, not only what the Exigencies of the People may require, but also force into the Trade of the Country, as much of his Coin, as he can put out of his Hands, with any Advantage to himself. And in order to do this, he will be able to allow large Premiums to those who will undertake to disperse his Tokens amongst the People, which he can afford to do by their wanting (as hath been already shewn) of *Intrinsick Value*. By which Means, the Country will be over-stock'd with this *base Coin*, and then, tho' too too late, its real Value will be found out, since that is the only Method those Persons will have of being reimbursed, who may be unfortunately seduced to part with their Gold or Silver, or valuable Commodities for it. For, indeed, it wou'd be highly unreasonable, that the Publick Revenues shou'd stand as a Security, for making good a Species of Money coined by private Persons: Which ought not to be expected, but when the *State* receives the Benefit of the Coinage.

And conformable to this good Policy, our Kings never granted any Power and Privilege of Coining Copper Halfpence and Farthings to private Persons, without taking sufficient Security, to prevent the great Mischief of having more of such base Coin introduced, than was necessary for carrying on the Business of the Nation. Thus in the Patents granted by King *Charles* 2d. and King *James* 2d. there is a Clause whereby it is provided, "That the "Patentees shou'd deliver unto any of the Subjects of *Ireland*, that shall find themselves *Surcharged* in the ordinary "Course of their Trade, with more of the said Copper

Halfpence

" Halfpence, than they can conveniently utter for their use
" or Occasions, the Sum of 20 Shilling *Ster.* in *Current Mo-*
" *ney*, for every Sum of Twenty Shillings in the said
" Copper Halfpence and so after that rate for all greater
" or lesser Sums, &c. In consequence of which Clause the Patentees established Persons in several Cities of the Kingdom, to Exchange their *Copper Halfpence* for *Current Money.* *

This Clause was a most Excellent Security against this great Mischief which is so justly apprehended from Mr. *Wood*'s Patent. For the Patentees were tyed down by *their own Interest*, not to pour in more of this Copper Money, than was necessary for carrying on the Trade of the Kingdom, least if their Coin came into Discredit, (as undoubtedly it must if the People found themselves *Surcharged* with it in the ordinary Course of their Trade) it shou'd be all pour'd back again, and by that means overwhelm their Project.

But in Mr. *Wood*'s Patent, there is no such Clause, and therefore he will have no other care about the Copper Money, than to pass it out of his Hands; and in order to do this, he will make use of what Means he can to force it into the Trade of the Nation, which is Manifest from part of Mr. *Finlay*'s Evidence before the Lords of his Majesty's most Honourable Privy Council in *Great Britain*, whereby that Gentleman declares he had contracted with Mr. *Wood* for 50,000 l. of his Money at 30 *per cent* Discount.

Which Contract shews Mr. *Wood* was resolv'd to dispose of more of his Copper, than there was a natural Demand for. For to dispose of what was only necessary for the use of the Kingdom, the very exigency of the People, wou'd naturally take it off his Hands, without any Premium. But his allowing 30 *per cent* Discount (or really any Discount at all) in the beginning of his Coinage, shews he proposed to force more than was necessary; and it is easy to conceive he would increase the Premium in Proportion as the Market wou'd be glutted, and the difficulty of dispersing his Coin wou'd be augmented; and thus the People wou'd be brought into that great Evil of being *Surcharged* with this base Money, without any possibility of being ever relieved.

But

---

* I am credibly inform'd, that, in consequence of this Clause, Sureties were enter'd by Recognizance in the Exchequer of *Ireland*

But perhaps, ſome People may imagine, that it is not abſolutely neceſſary, *Money* ſhould be made of *Gold* or *Silver*, but would perform the ſame uſes, if made of *Braſs*, *Copper*, *Tin*, or any thing elſe, that had an imaginary value aſign'd it by the Will of the Prince. Such Notions as theſe, might paſs well enough, with regard to a Country, to which the reſt of the World is unknown, or at leaſt where no Commerce with Foreigners is allow'd. There indeed, it would be no matter whether the *Money*, or what paſſes current in it as *Money*, were *Braſs*, or *Leather*, or *Shells*, or any ſuch trifling matter, provided the ſame may procure the People, all the Neceſſaries their own Country affords; and that Foreign Conveniencies and Commodities are entirely unknown to them. But to imagine that it were indifferent to uſe *Copper* or *Braſs*, inſtead of *Gold* and *Silver*, in a Country that has *Traffick* with other Nations, is a moſt extravagant Fancy; for Foreigners can only eſteem the *Money* of any Nation, according to its *determin'd Intrinſick Value*, and not with reſpect to any *Nominal Value*, one particular Nation gives it.

Therefore the Miſchiefs of Mr. *Wood*'s Coinage, muſt be conſider'd, as they ariſe from the want of *Intrinſick Value* in the Coin, (which *Intrinſick Value* alone, can give *Money* an univerſal Currency;) and from the Diſorders which neceſſarily attend the having too great a quantity of ſuch *Baſe Money*, in the current Caſh of the Nation: and theſe are to be computed, according to the *Quality* and *Quantity* of this Coin, attempted to be utter'd among us.

If Mr. *Wood* ſhou'd be contented to Coin 360 Tuns of *Copper*, which he is allow'd to do by the Patent, yet, as this quantity alone, would amount to 100.800 *l.* and that the *Intrinſick Value* of the Metal, is but 40.320 *l.* it appears, that there is by this means alone, a *real Loſs* to the Nation of 60.480 *l. tho' the terms of his Patent had been ſtrictly comply'd with*: For, as has been ſaid before, the Patent allows 30 *pence* to be coin'd out of every Pound of *Copper*; and the *Intrinſick Value* of the *Copper*, is but 12 *Pence per* Pound; wherefore there will always be a Defect of 3 fifths in what ever Sum is coin'd upon theſe Terms.

And, *that the Loſs would be much greater, in the manner the ſaid Halfpence have been coin'd*, moſt manifeſtly appear'd from the *Aſſays* made, and laid before the Houſes of Parliament, in *Ireland*; whereby it was prov'd, that ſome of thoſe

Halfpence, that were imported, with an intent to be utter'd in this Kingdom, run 72 to the Pound; at which rate the 360 Tun would amount to 120.960 *l.* and the *imediate Loss* to the Nation would be 80.460 *l.*

It must be confess'd, that either of those Sums, *is a Loss greater than this poor Country is able to bear*, or any the most nourishing Country would willingly bear, to gratify the Avarice of any undeserving Person whatsoever: Yet this is a Trifle, if compar'd with the Mischiefs that wou'd ensue: For if the loss of either of these Sums, was the only Evil, it would be then determin'd, and might perhaps be repair'd, by subsequent good Management: But in case this *Copper* had, through the *Avarice* of some, and the *Indolence* of others, obtain'd a Currency among us, the Mischiefs of it wou'd daily encrease, until at last the whole Affairs of the Nation wou'd be reduc'd to a deplorable Condition.

This will easily be conceiv'd, if it be remember'd that the Difference of 1 *l.* 3 *s.* 10 *d.* between 100 *l.* Value of *Gold Coin*, and 100 *l.* Value of *Silver Coin* of this Kingdom, compar'd with that of *England*, has had that Effect, that the greatest part of our *Silver Money* is, by that means, already taken out of the Country; and in a little time (it is apparent) the whole Silver Species must be drain'd away, if a timely remedy is not apply'd to it: with much more reason therefore, we ought to apprehend the fatal Consequences of this Patent, whereby there is a difference of 60 *per cent* created, between the *Imaginary Value* of this *Copper*, and the *lawful Money* of the Kingdom. For tho' in the Case of our *Silver Coin*, we loose it to our Disadvantage, yet the *Gold* that is brought instead thereof, amounts to near its *real Value*: But Mr. *Wood* being able to allow large Premiums, for dispersing his *Money*, if it had obtain'd any Credit among us, and the *Exchequer* had been permitted to support that Credit, we had reason to apprehend; he would by degrees, force in such quantities of his Coin, as wou'd draw away our *Gold* and *Silver*, and leave instead of them his *base Money*.

But, suppose Mr. *Wood*, to be so strictly Honest, as to keep within the terms of the Patent (which we have undeniable reasons to believe he is not) and that barely 100.000 *l.* should be forc'd into the Kingdom, according to the terms of the Patent: I shall consider the great Mischief, which even such a quantily would bring to the Nation; tho' I think

think it most plain, that, by Counterfiets and otherways, much greater Sums wou'd be introduced, before we could be sensible of them. And to do this, I must remind my Readers, that such a Sum of 100,000 *l.* of this Coin, would be, in *real Value*, equal to, only 40,000 *l.* of *lawful Money*.

In order to state this Matter rightly, I shall make use of some *Schemes*, that may be accepted, as exact enough to form any Reasonings upon; and which determine, the Number of Inhabitants in *Ireland*, their Annual Expence, and the means of their Subsistance.

The Inhabitants of *Ireland* are computed at *Two Millions* of Souls, and their Expence one with another, at 5 *l. per Annum* for each Person, which will make the Annual Expence of the Inhabitants amount to 10, 000, 000 *l.*

This necessary Expence is thus supply'd.

The Rental of *Ireland* is *per Annum*.	1, 600, 000	10, 000, 000
The Natural Encrease of Cattle, and the Product of the Land, by Husbandry &c. *per Annum*.	3, 200, 000	
And there is supply'd by other Industrious Arts, Manufactures, Trade, Commerce, Navigation, &c. about *per Annum*.	5, 200, 000	

To give Life to this Business, we have, as is generally computed, about 500,000 *l.* of ready Money in the Kingdom, which would not be sufficient, were it not that *Private Credit* serves instead of Money, and may be call'd *Artificial Money*, and this is computed equal to 1,000,000 *l.* which added to the *Natural Money*, makes 1,500,000 *l.* with a less Sum than which, it is hard to conceive how the Business of this Kingdom can be managed. And it's manifest, that the Rents and Product of the Land, the Labour and Industry of the People, are all measur'd by this Money: But this Money is of no greater *Intrinsick Value*, than Comparative with the Money of other Nations.

Now the *Real Money* of this Nation is 500, 000 *l.*

Of which we may ſuppoſe, that there remains of former Coinages in *Copper Money*, the Sum of } 25,000*l.*

And, if there ſhould be imported by Virtue of Mr. *Wood's* Patent in *Copper Money*, even only. } 100,000

The *Copper Money* of *Ireland* would be } 125,000

So that, of *Gold* and *Silver Money*, we muſt at moſt, have but } 375,000

} 500, 000 *l.*

Thus, this *unwieldy Copper Coin*, would be one fourth Part of the *Real* or *Natural Coin*; and it's eaſy to conceive this diſproportion'd Quantity of *Braſs Money*, would be a Clog to the whole Buſineſs of the Nation; for as the *Real Value* of this *Baſe Money* bears a Proportion to the *Imaginary Value* of it, but as 2 to 5, it is certain, Men of Underſtanding would make the ſame Difference between it, and the *Gold* and *Silver* Current in the Kingdom.

Wherefore this Difference diffuſing it ſelf through the whole Species of *Copper Money*, tho' the *Nominal Value* of it ſhould be ſuppos'd to be 125,000 *l.* yet in *Real Value* it would be only equal to 50,000 *l.* ſo that the want of *Intrinſick Value* in the *Copper Coin* is 75,000 *l.*

Which muſt have an Influence on the whole Caſh of the Nation, and conſequently create a Diffidence among the People of *Ireland*, which even the bare Apprehenſions of it, has already, in ſome Meaſure, effected, whereby at leaſt one fifth Part of the preſent Credit in the Country would be abated, and that is equal to } 200, 000*l.*

In all, to be deducted from the *Natural* and *Artificial Money* of the Nation. } 275, 000*l.*

So that, inſtead of a running Caſh and Credit, for managing the General Buſineſs of the Kingdom, to the Value of of 1,500,000 *l*, we ſhould only have 1,225,000 *l.* that is, the *Caſh* and *Credit* of the Nation would be leſſen'd of its preſent Value, by more than one ſixth Part. And ſince the Lands of *Ireland*, and the Encreaſe of them; the Labour and the Induſtry of the People (which are their whole Support) muſt all ſink in their Value, in Proportion as the Intrinſick

Value

Value of the Money, and Credit of the Nation are abated, it may be better conceiv'd than express'd, what the sad Consequences of this wou'd be.

We may be convinc'd of the Mischief attending such a Mixture in the *Current Cash*, if we please to examine the deplorable Condition *England* was falling into about the Years 1694 and 95, by Means of Part of the *Silver Coins* being debased by Clipping. To this Practice it was owing, that *Credit*, both *Private* and *Publick*, was put to a Stand; for by this Means a Traffick was carry'd on of exchanging the *Intrinsick* Riches of the Nation, with the Money so debased: Insomuch, that the *Legislature* was necessitated to interpose, and the Silver Money, that was subject to this Disorder, was call'd in at the publick Expence, and recoin'd.

Yet these great Disorders and Mischiefs were produc'd from no other Cause, than the Silver's being clip'd, whereby that *Proportion of Value* was destroy'd, which is so necessary to be maintained between the Current Coins of all *Trading Nations*. But in those Pieces of Silver, there was, *at the worst*, a greater Proportion of *Intrinsick Value* left, than is to be found in the *best* Copper Money of Mr. *Wood*. Which, considering the *Poverty* of the People of one Country, compared with the *flourishing Condition* of the other, must abundantly sooner influence us, than it could them: And it is allowed by every Body, that the *Clip'd Money* was an Evil, which, if not remedied, would have destroy'd the *Trade* of *England* in a short Time, and was a Distemper of that Consequence, that it required the utmost Skill of as *Great a King*, and as *Wise a Council*, as ever *England* had, to remedy it.

How necessary was it then for our *Poor Nation* to be careful not to involve it self in the like, nay, into greater Confusions! Was it for us to encourage the bringing in of a Parcel of *Copper Counters*, to pass instead of Money? And because they are call'd *Half-Pence* (when in Reality they are but *fifth Parts of Pence*) shall we receive them for our Valuable Goods, our *Gold* and our *Silver*?

Perhaps indeed, we should not be immediately sensible of the Evils that wou'd naturally attend this *Project*, as the *Bubble* seldom is of the Misfortunes he is falling into, until the *Sharper* has made his whole Advantage of him: Yet it is beyond all Doubt, the Effects of it would in Time de-

stroy

ſtroy us. This muſt be granted by any one who conſiders, as has been prov'd, that the People of *Ireland* would be deprived of at leaſt one ſixth Part of their preſent Means of Subſiſtance; and it is evident, this is an Evil of ſuch a Nature, as would in Time deſtroy any *Trading Country* whatſoever.

Should ever the Affairs of *Ireland* be reduc'd to this Paſs, the *Revenue* can never be ſuppos'd to produce as much as it does now. *That* muſt *riſe* and *fall*, in proportion as the Country grows *Rich* and *Populous*, or becomes *Poor* and *Diſpeopled*: So that upon the whole matter, it muſt appear to all intelligent Perſons, that, as theſe are the natural Conſequences, of introducing this *baſe Money* among us, ſo, *the Importing, and Uttering the Copper Farthings and Halfpence, made by vertue of the Patent granted to* William Wood, *will prove highly prejudicial to his Majeſty's Revenue, deſtructive of the Trade and Commerce of the Nation, and of moſt dangerous Conſequence to the Rights and Properties of the Subject.*

But perhaps, it may be ſaid, that ſince the Patent *doth not enforce this Currency of the Copper Money*, but hath left it, *to be receiv'd by ſuch only, as would Voluntarily and Willfully accept the ſame*; why ſhould all theſe Complaints be made againſt the Patent, and the Patentee? And why ſhould we raiſe to our ſelves, ſuch frightful Ideas, of the Conſequences which may attend this Project?

To this may be anſwer'd, That the Patent is in that part of it, *Juſt*, or rather *not Bad*, as it does not endeavour to take our *Liberty* from us; but ſurely, that does not hinder, but we may find ſuch Faults with the Project as it deſerves, and ſhew the evil Conſequences to the Nation, if the People ſhou'd be induc'd to take a quantity of theſe *Halfpence*, by any *Stratagems* or *Arts* whatſoever.

And ſince our *Houſes of Parliament*, have in the Wiſdom of their Councils, obſerv'd theſe Miſchiefs, it might have been expected, that ſuch Defference would be paid their Opinion, as that we ſhould never ſee the Teſtimony of three or four *obſcure Men*, put, any where, in Ballance with the *Reſolutions* and *Addreſſes* of the Repreſentatives of ſo *Great a Nation*.

But the Matter has prov'd otherways, and we have reaſon to apprehend, that ſtill there *may* be Attempts made, to enforce a Currency of this Coin. Several of thoſe Methods

did

did appear to the *Parliament.* They were well acquainted, that Mr. *Wood* allow'd *great Premiums* (as he could well do) to those, who should undertake to disperse his *Money*; and they were aware such Temptations, would have Power with Self-interested Men. They saw, *with Grief*, that some parts of the Patent might, by a *forc'd Construction*, be explain'd to intend, that this *Copper Money*, should be accepted in Payments to the *Crown*; and they very justly concluded, that if such Premiums were allowed for dispersing these *Tokens*, and that there should be so secure a Market for them, as the *Exchequer*, it would be difficult to prevent their obtaining a Currency among us: therefore as *Dutiful and Loyal Subjects*, and as *true Patriots* of their Country, they first represented the great Apprehensions they had of Danger from this Patent, and then, in order to avert the Evil, beseech'd *his Majesty* to direct, that this *Coin should not be receiv'd by the Officers, entrusted with the Receipt of his Revenue.*

As the *Great Council* of the Kingdom, it became them to do so: For it is their *Duty* to enquire into every thing that may Disturb the *Publick Tranquility*; and what ever Dangers they find Threatning, they are oblig'd to acquaint the *King* with them. Nor can there be a greater Instance of Respect to his *Majesty*, than, thus Humbly to Address his Throne, to pray him to give Orders to his Ministers, to prevent the Destruction of his People, by so mild and just a Method, as forbiding them to allow a Currency to these *Halfpence* in the *Exchequer*; which all Men know, was only beseeching his *Majesty*, to Order the *Officers of his Revenue*, to Act conformable to the *Laws of the Land.*

It is therefore the Duty of every particular Person of this Nation, to concur with the Endeavours used by *our Parliament*, to avert the *Evil* of this Coinage; and since we have a Right to refuse *this Coin*, let every one of us *continue* to reject it, and let us not be tempted, by Views of *private Advantage*, to involve *our Country*, in the Miseries which must of course be brought upon it, if this *Brass Money* should obtain a Currency among us. The good Consequences that have *already* attended the Opposing of this Patent, ought to Encourage us in *Persevering* in it: For since the quantity allow'd by the Patent to be coin'd, is already reduced to 40,000 *l.* we have reason to expect upon a *continued unanimous Opposition*, to the Patentee, and humble Application to *his Majesty*, it will be wholy laid aside. But,

But, before I conclude, I shall beg leave to compare the Patent, for Coining *Copper Money* for *Ireland*, granted by *King Charles* the 2d, and afterwards renew'd to Mr. *Knox*, by *King James* the 2d. with this granted to Mr. *Wood*, and to examine the *Assay*, made of Mr. *Wood's Coinage* in the Tower of *London*, upon the Considerations of both which, the Lords of the Council of *Great Britain*, ground their Reasons, in their Report to his Majesty, for justifying Mr. *Wood*'s Patent.

It has been said, and the Lords of the Council of *Great Britain*, seem to believe, " That the Care and Caution made " use of, in this Patent granted to Mr. *Wood*, by proper Con- " ditions, Checks, and Comptrols, have effectually provid- " ed, that the *Copper Money* coin'd for *Ireland* by Virtue of " this Patent, shou'd far exceed the like Coinages for *Ireland*, " in the Reigns of his Majesty's Royal Predecessors" and this, they say, " is evidently prov'd by the Tryals and Assays " made of the fineness, Value and Weight of this *Copper Mo- " ney*, and the goodness thereof compar'd with former Coi- " nages of *Copper Money* for *Ireland*. But before I examine this Assay, I will compare the Patents, in some of their Circumstances, together.

Mr. *Wood*, by his Patent, has a Power given him, of Coining 360 Tuns of *Copper* for *Ireland*, and he is allow'd to make 30 Pence out of every Pound Weight of *Copper*. By the Patent granted by *King Charles* 2d. and renewed by *King James* 2d. to Mr. *Knox*, the Patentees had liberty to Coin such quantities of *Copper Halfpence*, as they could conveniently Issue, and they had liberty to make 32 Pence out of a Pound of *Copper*. In this Mr. *Knox* seems to have had the advantage of Mr. *Wood*, in as much as he had liberty of Coining 2 Pence more, out of a Pound of *Copper*, than Mr. *Wood* has; but it will appear far otherwise, if we consider, that in the time of the former Coinages, *Copper*, of the same fineness, with what is now worth, in *Ireland*, 12 d. per Pound, cou'd not be bought for less than 18 d. per Pound. According to which Difference in the price of the Material, the Patent granted to Mr. *Wood*, ought to have regulated his Coinage at 26 Pence per Pound of *Copper*, and he would have the same Benefits, that were allow'd to the Patentees by the former Patents.

But

But Mr. *Wood* is allow'd to make 30 d. out of a Pound of *Copper*, therefore, he has a superiour Advantage given him of 4 d. per Pound, which upon 360 Tuns, amounts to 13,440 *l.* and hereby it is plain, the Patent granted to Mr. *Wood*, is not equally advantagious to the People of *Ireland*, with that granted to Mr. *Knox*.

But further, let it be suppos'd, that the Comptroler appointed by Mr. *Wood's* Patent, takes effectual care of the goodness, and fineness of the *Copper*, of which his *Halfpence and Farthings*, are made. Yet the care taken in the former Patents, was more effectual; for, tho' there was *no* express *Provision made, for the goodness and fineness of the Copper*, yet, there was a more effectual Remedy, provided against all the Mischiefs, that could attend that Coinage, as appears by the Clause of Mr. *Knox's* Patent, which is already mention'd (*Page* 7) which was an effectual Remedy against *the pouring in too great a quantity of Copper Money*, which is the great Evil to be dreaded. And thus, the former Patentees were bound by their own Interest, to take care of the *quality* of the *Halfpence*, and *quantity* to be utter'd; whereas Mr. *Wood* is not properly restrain'd, having no more to say to his *Halfpence and Farthings*, after they have once pass'd the Comptrolers Inspection. And of what little Security this Restriction is on him, I shall hereafter have occasion to take Notice.

It is also worth observing, that, in the Patent granted to Mr. *Knox*, there is a farther care taken, that that Coinage shou'd not prove Mischievous to the People of *Ireland*; for his then Majesty did " Covenant and Promise, that if, dur- " ing the term thereby granted, it should fall out to be con- " venient, *for the good of his Subjects*, that any Alteration " should be made in the *Metal*, or in the *Stamp* of the said " *Copper Halfpence*, that, in such case, he would *Authorize* " *by Proclamation*, such Alteration, as shou'd be found *fit* " and *convenient*: Whereby it is plain, that, by this Patent, a Power was still reserv'd in the Crown, to prevent, by Proclamation, any Evil Consequences, that might have attended that Coinage, which, it's manifest, was only intended *for the good of the Subjects of Ireland*: Whereas we are told, that by the Patent to Mr. *Wood*, his Majesty has divested himself of all Power, of relieving his Subjects, from the dangers of this Coinage, unless it be by a Writ of *Scire facias*; and if

C it

it be really so, it would seem, as if this Patent was, rather a Grant in favour of the Patentee, than for the good of the People of *Ireland.*

It has been also said, " that the Money coin'd by virtue " of the Patent granted to *John Knox*, is made, and declared " to be *current Coin* of the Kingdom of *Ireland.* I have therefore very carefully examin'd that Patent, and I cannot find it contains any thing that can be explain'd this way, only the Clause, whereby it is " ordain'd, that the *Copper* " *Halfpence*, made by vertue of the said Patent, should pass, " and be generally used, between Man and Man, as Money " for the value of *Halfpence*. But this is not an attempt to enforce a *Currency* of this *Coin*, or to make it *lawful Money*, contrary to the *known Laws* of the Kingdom. It is only a Licence, *that those Halfpence shall be used generally between Man and Man*; and this will appear to have been the intent of the Patent, on reading the Clause mentioned in Page (7) wherein a Difference is made, between this *Copper Money*, and the *Current Money* of the Kingdom; which Difference wou'd have been unnecessary, if it was intended, that the *Copper Money* shou'd have been made the *Current Money* of *Ireland.*

And the whole Purport of the said Patent, confirms this Opinion: For in the Clause immediately following, that which I have just now cited, his Majesty declares, that " to the " intent that *just Exchange* (which is provided for in the former Clause ") may be maintain'd, and consequently *all in-* " *conveniencies* avoided, which might *otherways* happen to " *his Subjects*, coutrary to his *gracious Intention and Mean-* " *ing*; his Will and Pleasure therefore is, that there be from " time to time, a convenient quantity of the said *Halfpence*, " sent to as many Cities, Burroughs, Corporate and Market " Towns, and other Places within the Realm of *Ireland*, " as the Patentees shall think fit, and necessary for the use " and occasions of the People of *Ireland*, and the same *Cop-* " *per Halfpence*, to be left in the Hands of some *discreet Per-* " *son or Persons* in the said Cities, *&c.* together with sufficient " Means, for the *Re-change* of the said *Halfpence*". And when *his Majesty*, in the same Patent, " Wills and Requires " his *Chief Governors*, &c. for the time being, to endeavour, " that the said *Copper Halfpence*, may freely pass in use be- " tween Man and Man"; it is expresly said, " *in the way*

" of

" *of Exchange, as is before expreſs'd*". Whereby it is Manifeſt, that it was never intended, this Coin ſhould be made the *Current Money* of the Kingdom: But was only to paſs *by way of Exchange*, as is before expreſs'd; that is, the Patentees to *Exchange* them for *Gold* and *Silver*, (which are the only *lawful Money* of this Kingdom) whenever the ſame would be requir'd, and this the *Chief Governors*, &c. were commanded by the ſaid Patent to ſee duely perform'd.

I muſt beg leave further to Remark, that the Patent granted to Mr. *Knox*, was order'd to be enrol'd in the Rolls of the *High Court of Chancery* in *Ireland*, whereas this granted to Mr. *Wood*, is enrol'd in *England*; and tho' this may ſeem no material Difference, yet I cannot forbear looking upon it, as a matter of very great Conſequence; for it is a Queſtion, whether a Writ of *Scire facias* will lye in *Ireland* againſt this Patent, and it ſeems very agreeable to Reaſon, that a Tryal on ſuch a Writ, if the Patent cou'd not be any otherwiſe vacated, ought to be had in *this Kingdom*, rather than in *England*. But this, and the Inconveniencies that might attend ſuch a Tryal, in caſe it cou'd be had in *Ireland*, on this Patent granted under the great Seal of *England*, and enrol'd in that Kingdom, I muſt leave to the Conſideration of thoſe who are learn'd in the Laws of the Land.

Upon the whole Matter, I think it plainly appears, that the Patent granted to Mr. *Wood*, *is not equally Beneficial to the Kingdom of Ireland*, with the former Patents; and, *that from the foregoing great and eſſential Differences*, whereby *it ſeems ſufficiently juſtified, that Care and Caution was* not *uſed in granting the Letters Patent to Mr.* Wood.

And now I ſhall Examine the Aſſay made of Mr. *Wood's* Coinage, in the Tower of *London*; and to do this the better, I ſhall beg leave to annex a Coppy of the Report thereof, to theſe Papers.

By this Report, it is Evident, that there was but *one Species* of Mr. *Wood's* Halfpence *Aſſay'd*, viz. thoſe which were coin'd between the 25th of *March*, 1723. and *March* 28th, 1724. bearing on the Reverſe, *HIBERNIA* ſitting with a *Harp* by her left Side, and the Date of the Year. Theſe might have the Qualities certified, and the *Fraud* charg'd on the Patentee, ſtill ſubſiſt. For the Aſſays made in *Ireland*, and laid before the *Houſes of Parliament*, in the Month of *September*, 1723, were on different Species imported into

Ireland

Ireland, in order to be utter'd, and most of them were coin'd in the Yeer 1722, as appears by their Dates, and several of the Impressions on the Reverse, were different from the Species that was try'd in the Tower of *London.*

The Persons concern'd in the Assay made in *Ireland*, were examined by a Committee of the *Whole House of Commons* in a most solemn Manner; a Method not observed, on the other side the Water.

And, to the End there should be no Ground given, for an Imputation that light Pieces were pick'd up for the Tryal in *Ireland*, but that the same should be made with all the Candour imaginable; I am well assured, that the Assay made in *Ireland*, was proved by several Tryals on large Parcels of Mr. *Wood*'s *Half-pence*, then lying in the Stores of His Majesty's Custom-House in *Dublin*, and which were imported from *Bristol*: So that this Assay made by Order of *the House of Commons of* Ireland, can't, with any Shew of Reason, be call'd, in Question, but certainly carries better Evidence of Truth with it, than any other Assay whatsoever.

By this Assay it appear'd, that *Half-pence* of four different Impressions, and of much less weight, than was requir'd by Patent were imported into *Ireland* before *September* 1723, of which, Specimens are in the Custody of the Clerk of *the House of Commons.* But there was only one Sort produced before the Gentlemen employ'd to make the Assay in the Tower of *London*; which could not have happen'd, if the Comptroller had perform'd his Duty; for then he would have raken *Tryal Pieces* out of each different Parcel that was coin'd during the whole Time, and then the *different Impressions and Dates* would have appear'd, to the Gentlemen who were appointed to make the Assay in the Tower of *London.*

But this having, in all Appearance, been contrived, by Mr. *Wood* and his Accomplices, in order to deceive the Lords of the Council, as in Effect it has done, it may be allow'd that other Contrivancies that could serve to the same End, were put in Practice: And then, it is natural to believe, the *heaviest Pieces* were chosen out of Mr. *Wood*'s *Coinage*, for this Tryal.

But Mr. *Wood* has imposed on the Lords of the Council in another most Material Point, and in this too the Comptroler is very deeply concern'd with Mr. *Wood.* This will appear by by comparing the Report of the Committee of Council, with the Report of the Aſſay. In the former it is ſaid; "That "the Comptrolers Accounts of the Quantities of *Half-pence* "*and Farthings* coin'd, agreed with Mr. *Wood*'s Account, "amounting to 59 Tuns, 3 Hundred, 1 Quarter, 11 Pound "and 4 Ounces;" Whereas by the Report made of the Aſſay it appears, that, "from Lady-day 1723, to the 28th of "*March* 1724, there was that Quantity coin'd."

From hence it is plain, that no Account has been return'd of the Coinage in the Year 1722, and the Lords of the Council were made to believe, that the Quantities of *Copper* coin'd amounted in the whole only to the aforeſaid Weight, and in Tale to 17,000 *l.* whereas by the Report of the Aſſay it appears, that Quantity and Sum was coin'd between the 25th of *March* 1723, and the 28th of *March* 1724.

And ſeeing that the Patent was enroll'd in the Rolls of the High-Court of *Chancery* in *England*, on the 12th Day of *July* 1722, the Patentee had full eight Months Time to coin in, before the 25th of *March* 1723: In which Time, at the Rate of 100 Tuns for the firſt Year, as preſcrib'd by the Patent, he muſt have coin'd 66 Tun at leaſt, which at 2 *s.* 6 *d.* per Pound amounts to 18,480 *l.* and this was intirely withheld from the Knowledge of the Lords of the Council, ſo that Mr. *Wood* had coin'd 35,480 *l.* in Tale, when he and the Comptroller pretended there was only 17,000 *l.* coin'd.

Now, this has been an Impoſition of a moſt high Nature, and it is enough to demonſtrate, that there is little Expectation, of ever being able to ſet Limits to a Beneficial Coinage, entruſted in private Hands, by the Means of any Comptroller: and therefore all Propoſals from Mr. *Wood* of limiting his Coinage to 40,000 *l.* or to any other Sum, are Amuſements that Wiſe Men will never be deceiv'd by.

I muſt further beg Leave to remark, that, tho' it is ſaid in the Report, "that the *Half-pence* and *Farthings* coin'd by "Mr. *Wood*, when compar'd with the *Copper Money* coin'd "for *Ireland* in the Reigns of King *Charles* IId, King "*James* IId, and King *William* and Queen *Mary*, conſi-"derably exceeds them all in Weight, *&c.*" Yet this is no Way to be conſider'd in the preſent Queſtion.

For it is of no Conſequence to examine the intrinſick Value of our *preſent Half-pence*, becauſe, as the People of *Ireland*

land are *not ſurcharg'd* with them, they are generally eſteemed for the Conveniency of making ſmall Payments, and, until this Attempt of Mr. *Wood*, we have not been in Danger of being *ſurcharg'd* with *Copper Money*; but when this Danger, of having a diſproportioned Quantity brought in, did threaten us; it was then, as has been already ſaid, the Concern of every Body to compute the Miſchiefs that might attend it, by the Want of Intrinſick Value in the Coin.

Upon this Matter of the Aſſay made of Mr. *Wood's Copper Money*, I muſt alſo take Notice, that tho' the *Copper* of which Mr. *Wood's Half-pence* are made, ſhould be allow'd to be, of the ſame Goodneſs and Value with that, of which the *Copper Money* is coin'd in his Majeſty's Mint for *England*; yrt the Quantity of Money that is allowed to be coin'd out of a Pound of Copper for *Ireland*, is not in a juſt Proportion to what is coin'd for *England*.

For, if the ſame Proportion that is obſerv'd between the *Silver Money* of each Nation, was maintain'd in the Copper Coin, then there ought not to be made out of one Pound of Copper for *Ireland*, but 25 Pence and 2 thirds of a Penny. For as 24 Pence of Silver Money of *England*, yields 26 Pence in *Ireland*, ſo 23 Pence, the Quantity of Half-pence made out of a Pound of *Copper* for *England*, is equal to 25 Pence and 2 Thirds of a Penny, the Quantity that ought to be made for *Irleand*.

But as Mr. *Wood* has Liberty to make 30 Pence out of a Pound of Copper for *Iraland*, ſo he has an Advantage of 4 Pence and 1 Third of a Penny on every Pound of *Copper*, more than what is got by the *Copper Coinage* for *England*; and this upon 360 Tuns, amounts to 14,000 *L*. and by this Means, the Difference between the *Copper Money* of *England*, and the *Copper Money* of *Ireland*, would prove 32 and a half per Cent, and as the Difference of the Value of Money, is one of the chief Reaſons of the riſing of Exchange between two Nations, it is manifeſt, that if this Coin of Mr. *Wood* had been forc'd upon us; the Exchange between *England* and *Ireland* would be raiſed to at leaſt 30 per Cent, whereas for ſome Years paſt, it has, by a Medium kept at about 10 per Cent.

And if the Exchange ſhould thus come to be raiſed, it would produce moſt fatal Conſequences to the *Trade*, and generally to every other *Buſineſs* of the Nation.

That

That those of my Readers, who are unacquainted with matters of this Nature, may be able to judge of the Disadvantages, such high Exchange would produce: I must inform them, that the causes of the rise and fall of Exchange, are; either the variation of the Price of the Coin in any Country, or the Demand that happens to be in one Country, for Money in another, or, sometimes both those *Causes* meeting together.

Now 'tis well known, that the great Number of *Irish* Landlords, the Pensioners and great Officers on our Civil and Military Establishments, who live in *England*; and the Income of our Post Office, and some other Portions of Publick Money, which are yearly remitted to that Country, do all together occasion a great Demand for Money in *England*: And if a Variation of our Coin should concurr with this, it is easy to conceive that the *Exchange* would rise to the Heigth of the *greatest Difference* between the Money of *England and Ireland.*

It has been already shewn that the *Nominal Value* of the Silver Money in *Ireland*, compared to the Value of the Silver Money of *England*, is as 108,333, to 100, and *Gold* in *Ireland* compared to *Gold* in *England*, is as 109,525 to 100, so that the *Exchange* between *England* and *Ireland*, holding by a Medium, for some Time past, at 10 *per Centum*, confirms our Observation that the *Exchange* must rise to the *greatest Difference* between the *Nominal Value* of our Coins. Wherefore as the *Brass* Money intended to be forced upon us by Mr. *Wood* (tho' he should make it conformable to the Rules of his Patent) would be 32 and an half *per Centum* worse than the *Brass Money*, and near 70 *per Cent.* worse than the *Silver Money* of *England*, it is easy to conceive that the Price of *Exchange* between *England* and *Ireland*, would be raised to at least 30 *per Cent.* if this *Brass* Coinage should be allowed to take Effect.

So that, if in carrying on the *general Trade* and *Business* of the Nation, the Bills drawn between *England* and *Ireland* amount to 2,000,000*l. per Ann. Irish Money*, and that *Exchange* should be at 30 *per Cent.* then this Sum would be discharged by 1,538,462 *l, English Money.* Whereas now that *Exchange* holds at 10 *per Cent.* that Sum produces 1,818,182 *l. English Money.* Thus by the raising of *Exchange* there wou'd be lost to the Nation 279,720 *per Ann. English*

Money

Money, which at 30 *per Cent.* would be equal to 363,636*l.* *Irish Money per Annum.*

I would not have my Reader imagine, that the Loss which *Ireland* would sustain by this Means must redound to the Profit of *England*, for it is far otherwise. The Merchants of *Ireland* are for the most Part only Factors for other Countries; and Foreigners both to *England* and *Ireland*, wou'd gain the greatest Share, in the Advantages which all the World would have by a Mismanagement of this Kind, in the Affairs of *Ireland.* And tho' some *particular Persons* in *England* might gain by such Confusions, yet it would be directly opposite to the general Interest of that Country.

I might prove this by many Arguments; but at this Time I shall content my self with examining how this Matter of the *Exchange* will affect the Money that is remitted to *England*, to pay the annual Demand that Country has on this Kingdom.

This Demand may be computed at 500,000 *l. per Annum Irish Money*, which when *Exchange* is at 10 *per Cent.* is paid by 454,545 *English* Money; but if Exchange should be raised to 30 *per Cent*, than it would be paid by 384,615 *l. English* Money: So that the loss by this means alone to the *Irish* Landlords, the Pensioners, and great Officers on the Civil and Military Lists of *Ireland*, who spend their large Incomes in *England*, and in the Revenues of the Post-Office, &c. would be 69,930 *l. English* Money *per Annum*, equal to 90,909 *l. Irish* Money. That is, more than the 6th part of their whole Incomes would be destroy'd by this means. And it is worth observing, that, this confirms our Computation of the like Proportion of loss to the whole People of *Ireland*, in case *this Brass Money* should obtain a *Currency* among us, as in Page (12.)

I have been the longer in Examining the aforementioned Patents, and the Assay made of Mr. *Wood's Copper Halfpence* in *London*, they being the Foundations, on which the Lords of the Council form'd their Opinion, that Mr. *Wood* had not deceiv'd his Majesty, in obtaining this Grant; That he had on his part duly perform'd the Covenants he had enter'd into; and that this Coinage was Beneficial to the People of *Ireland*: But having put these Matters in a fair Light, I hope they'll now appear in another manner, than they did to their Lordships.

For

For my part, I can never suppose, but the *Interest* of *England* and that of *Ireland*, as now establish'd, shou'd be so united, that it may always remain as a Maxim in Politicks, that *Ireland* cannot be destroy'd without bringing a most sensible Damage to the Affairs of *England*. And I'm perswaded, the Affection of *the King* is so very great towards his Subjects in this Country, that he never would willingly suffer them to be ruin'd by the Projects of *Avaritious Men*; nor can it enter into my Mind, that any of the *Ministers*, who are entrusted with the immediate Management of the Affairs of *Great Britain*, did advise the granting this Patent, out of a desire to hurt his Majesty's most dutiful Subjects of *Ireland*.

I'm rather of Opinion, that Mr. *Wood* found means, to make it be believ'd, that it was really for the Service of the People of *Ireland*, that this Patent should take Place. And now that it appears Mr. *Wood* has deceiv'd *his Majesty* in this Grant, those Ministers who (when they thought it was for the good of this Kingdom) were most Instrumental in obtaining this Patent, will be the readiest (it is to be hoped) to cause it to be vacated, since its manifestly destructive of the common Interest of *his Majesty* and *his Subjects*.

I shall conclude this Paper with a *Speech* made by Queen *Elizabeth*, in Answer to an *Address* of Thanks from the *House of Commons* of *England*, upon *her Majesty*'s Publishing a Proclamation, declaring several *Patents* to be *Null and Void*, which *she* had granted to private Persons (who under the Colour of *publick good*, but in reality to the great *Damage*, of the Kingdom) had obtain'd them, for the sole Privilege and Liberty of vending some particular sorts of Wares.

And when I have desired, it may be consider'd, that few *Princes* had asserted the *Rights of the Crown*, with a higher Hand than *she* did, I shall leave my Reader with this *Speech*, to make a proper Application of it. The *Speech* is as follows.

Gentlemen,

I Owe you my best Thanks and Acknowledgements for your Respect towards me, not only for your good Inclination, but those clear and publick Expressions thereof, which have discover'd themselves, in retrieving me from a Mistake, into which I have been betray'd; *not so much by the Faults of my Will, as the Error of my Judgment. This had unavoidably drawn a Blemish upon me, (who account the safety of my*

People my chief Happiness,) had you not made me acquainted with the practice of those lude Harpies and Horse-leeches. *I would sooner loose my Hand or Heart, than ever consent to allow such Privileges to* Engrosers, *as* may turn *to the* detriment to to my People. *I am not so blinded with the lustre of a Crown, as to let the* Scale of Justice *be weigh'd down, by that of an* Arbitrary Power. *The gay Title of a* Prince, *may deceive such as know nothing of the Secret of Governing, as a gilded Pill may impose upon the Patient: But I am not one of those* unwary Princes; *for I am very sensible, that I ought to govern for the* publick good, *and not regard my own particular, and that I stand accountable to another, a greater Tribunal. I account my self very Happy, that by God's Assistance, I have enjoy'd so* prosperous a Government *in all respects, and that he has blessed me with* such Subjects, *for whom I could be contented to lay down my Crown and my Life. I must entreat you, that let* others *be Guilty of what Faults or Misdemeanours soever, they may not, through any Misrepresentation be laid at my Door. I hope the Evidence of a good Conscience will, in all respects, bear me out. You cannot be* Ignorant, *that the* Servants of Princes, *have too often, an Eye to their* own Advantage; *that their Faults are often concealed from their Notice, and that they cannot, if they wou'd, inspect all things, when the weight and Business of a whole Kingdom lyes on their Shoulders.*

A

A Coppy of the *Report* made by Sir *Isaac Newton*, *Edw Southwel*, and *John Scroope*, Esqs; of the *Assay* made of Mr. *Wood's Copper Money.*

To the Right Honourable the Lords Commissioners of his Majesty's Treasury.

May it please your Lordships,

ACCORDING to your Lordship's Order, the *Pix* of the *Copper Money* coined at *Bristol* by Mr. *Wood* for *Ireland*, has been opened, and tryed before us, at his Majesty's Mint in the Tower: And, *by the Comptrolers Account*, to which Mr. *Wood* agreed, there has been coined *from Lady-day*, 1723. *to March*, 28th. 1724. in Halfpence, 55 Tuns, 5 Hundred, 3 Quarters, and 12 Ounces, and in Farthings 3 Tuns, 17 Hundred, 2 Quarters, 10 Pounds, 8 Ounces, Averdupois; *the whole Coinage amounting to* 59 *Tuns*, 3 *Hundred*, 1 *Quarter*, 11 *Pounds, and* 4 *Ounces*. And by Specimens of this Coinage, which have from time to time been taken from several Parcels coined, and sealed up in Papers, and put into the *Pix*; we found, that 60 *Halfpence* weighed 14 Ounces Troy, and 18 Penny weight, which is about a quarter of an Ounce, above 1 Pound weight Averdupois, and that 30 Farthings weighed 3 Ounces, and 3 quarters of an Ounce Troy, and 46 Grains, which is also above the weight required by his Patent. We found also, that both *Halfpence* and *Farthings*, when heated red hot, spread thin under the Hammer without Cracking, as your Lordships may see by the pieces now laid before your Lordships. But altho the Copper was very good, and the Money one piece with another was full weight, yet the single pieces were not so equally coined, in the weight, as they shou'd have been.

We found also, that 32 old Halfpence coined for *Ireland*, in the Reigns of King *Charles* 2d. King *James* 2. and King *William* 3. and Queen *Mary*, *and produced by* Mr. *Wood*,

weighed

weighed 6 Ounces and 8 Penny weight Troy, that is 105 Grains and an half a piece one with another. They were much worn, and if about 6 or 7 Grains be allowed to each of them, one with another, for loſs of their weight by wearing, the Copper Money coined for *England*, in the Reign of King *William*, being already as much lightened by wearing, they might at firſt weigh about half a Pound Averdupois, whereas 30 of thoſe coined by Mr. *Wood*, are to be of that weight, They were alſo made of bad Copper. Two of thoſe coined in the Reign of King *Charles* 2d. waſted much in the Fire, and then ſpread thin under the Hammer, but not ſo well without cracking as thoſe of Mr. *Wood*. Two of thoſe coined in the Reign of King *James* 2d. waſted more in the Fire, and were not malleable when red hot. Two of thoſe coined in the Reign of King *William* and Queen *Mary*, waſted ſtill more in the Fire, and turn'd to an unmalleable Subſtance, like a Cinder; as your Lordſhips may ſee by the Pieces now laid before you.

By the *Aſſays* we reckon the Copper of Mr. *Wood*'s Halfpence and Farthings to be of the ſame goodneſs, and value, with the Copper, of which the Copper Money is coined in the King's Mint for *England*, worth in the Market, about 12 or 13 d. per Pound weight Averdupois. And the Copper of which the Halfpence were coined for *Ireland*, in the Reigns of King *Charles*, King *James*, and King *William*, to be much inferior in value, the mixture being unknown, and not bearing the Fire, for converting it to any other uſe, until it be refined.

The *Halfpence* and *Farthings* in the *Pix*, coined by Mr. *Wood*, had on one ſide, the Head of the King, with this Inſcription *GEORGIUS DEI GRATIA REX*, and on the other Side, a Woman Siting, *with a Harp by her left Side*, and above her, this Inſcription, *HIBERNIA, with the Date*. The *Halfpence* coined in the Reigns of King *Charles*, King *James*, and King *William*, had, on one Side, the Head of King *Charles*, King *James*, or King *William* and Queen *Mary*, and on the Reverſe, a Harp crowned.

All which Facts we moſt humbly Repreſent to your Lordſhips. *April*, 27*th*. 1724.

FINIS.

REMARKS UPON MR. WOOD'S COYN

Bibliographical note:

this facsimile has been made from a copy in the Beinecke Library of Yale University (NZ.724c)

REMARKS
UPON
Mr. *WOOD*'s Coyn

AND

PROCEEDINGS.

Salus Populi, Suprema lex est.

By Sir *Michael Creagh.*

DUBLIN:

Printed by *William Wilmot* on the *Blind-Key*, 1724.

REMARKS

UPON

Mr. *WOOD*'s COIN, &c.

THAT the Publick or Common Welfare of the People, has been the View and Aim of all Law-Givers, and Law-Makers, that ever were, is Evident by all Divine and Profane Histories, as of *Moses* the first Law-Giver, under God, of the People of *Israel*, and *Minos*, *Lycurgus*, *Numa Pomphilius* in *Crete*, *Lacedemonia*, and *Rome*, or *Italy*. It is therefore Doubtless, That the Publick Welfare upon all Occasions is Preferrable to all Particular or Private Interests, and that all humane Industry, Wit and Reasoning deem'd to be opposite to the Publick Welfare, ought to be opposed and rejected. The Origin of Kings, Princes, Governors, and Governments, Confirm this Truth from *Nimrod* through all the Revolutions and Changes of Governments in the World to this Day.

Experience and History have sufficiently shewed us the ill Consequences, when Kings, Princes, Governors, or their Ministers are thought to in-croach

croach upon the Publick Welfare or Safety, it's therefore the Duty of all good Subjects and Lovers of their King, and Country, to Endeavour as much as in them lyes, to prevent any fatal Effects to Either: By Advice and Council, if in no other Capacity, Experience lets us often see, what Effects a common Notion, whether well, or ill Grounded, has made upon Peoples minds, and what Disorders and Misfortunes have followed thereupon, to the very overturning of Governments, with Blood and Massacre, in a belief that the Publick or common Welfare required it; this Truth is so well known, that its needless to come to Particulars.

If a Nation in general Presuppose, or are perswaded, that an Affair in Agitation is highly Prejudicial to their Welfare, Trade, Commerce, Liberties, and Properties, though in Effect it may not be so, yet in such a Case I am perswaded all Men of good Sense will admit that Prudence requires a management to Prevent a greater Evil, Especially when the Situation of Worldly Affairs absolutely require it.

This is the Case as to Mr. *Wood*'s Half-pence coyn'd, or to be coyn'd, for this Kingdom of *IRELAND*.

This whole Kingdom, (except a few of his Friends) are perswaded, his Patent will be their Ruin: This Supposition is Grounded upon two Points, the first is, That the uttering said Halfpence, being an Affair whereof the Profit must be for particular Persons; and the loss for the Generality, or the Publick; all the Frauds and Deceits that can be practis'd, will be Smother'd among those who are Gainers, by said Affair, and the Publick must Bear and Suffer the Loss. There is a plain Evidence hereof already in this case, for if the Publick Welfare be duly Consider'd, the Welfare of one of His Majesty's Dominions ought to be Cherish'd as well as that of the other, why then are not Mr. *Wood's* best Half-pence made equal in in Value, and Weight, with the *English* Half-pence coyned for *England*, and that they are not so, is Visible as any one may find by Experience, or Tryal. In the next place, its plain and notorious, that a great Number of what Half-pence of Mr. *Wood's* Fabrick, are come into this Kingdom, differ in the Weight alone, setting aside the Quality of the Brass, One and Twenty Grains, for they have been so often Weighed: Now seeing its Evident and Plain that there is already a Deceit and Cheat in said Coyn, as to the Weight, besides the Intrinsick Value of the Brass, as has been so often Tryed, and found so by both Houses of Parliament in this Kingdom; and others, how Visible and Plain must it appear to all the World, That Mr. *Wood* and his Friends have Imposed upon Sir *Isaac Newton*, Mr. *Southwell*, and Mr. *Scrope*, by bringing them Specimens of said Coyn, and Tryal-Pieces so different in Value and Weight from what is daily seen in *Ireland*, as I have already mentioned, and thus said Gentlemen, and the Right Honourable the Lords of the Committee, of His Majesty's most Honourable Privy Council are missed, and imposed upon, by a Supposition,

position, That Mr. *Wood* has performed his Covenants, and consequently, That his Patent ought to take Effect, whereas its Evident, there are Thousands of his Half-pence now in *Ireland*; which prove the Contrary. Now there is no Doubt but Mr. *Wood* will pretend, That this bad Coyn is none of his, to which can be easily Objected, that it can be no other but his Coyn, for it would not be worth any Bodies while to Counterfeit a Coyn, not at all Courant, and not known whether it ever would be Courant, besides, That its Notorious, these very Half-pence were of the first that came for *Ireland*, by way of *Cork*, and otherwise, Witness the Essays made by the Honourable House of Commons, of *Ireland*'s Directions, and this Deceit being already so Plain and Visible, notwithstanding all his Proofs and Evidences, from the *Pitts*, and Comptroller, &c. of *Bristol*, how easy its to be Comprehended, Thar the Deceit will not be at an End, when he has full Power and Authority to Act as he thinks fit. The Second Point is, That in a Case, where the Profit is to accrue to particular Persons, and the Loss to the Publick; all Contrivances for Lucre and Gain, cannot fail of taking Effect, we have had a Woful Example hereof in the late Directors of the *South-Sea* Company, when it was plain, That of above 30 in Number, (all reputed to be honest Men) there was not one found to be so: What wonder is it then, That the People of *Ireland*, (who had their share of the *South-Sea* Losses) should be under an Apprehension, not only of getting Forty Thousand Pounds, when Twenty would suffice,

ſuffice, and that moſt part in bad Coyn, as already appears, but that under the Notion of coyning but Forty Thouſand, he may Coyn in *England*, *Ireland*, and *Scotland*, for *Ireland* alone, above 200 Thouſand, in a Clandeſtine way, and ſo bring all that Braſs upon this Nation, in ſuch a Meaſure, as to ſweep away all their Silver and Gold, by giving 30, 40, and 50 Shillings in Braſs, for a Guinea in Gold, or 23 Shillings in Silver, and ſo make the People more unhappy, and raiſe the Price of all Goods, to the utter Deſtruction of the Poor; and Ruin of all Trade, worſe than in King *James*'s Braſs-Money Time. Experience ſhews us, That the longer the World ſubſiſts, the more Accute the People grow, and as we are naturally more Prone to Evil than Good, our Accuteneſs tends more that way, contrary to all Laws Divine, and Humane, and that firſt Law of Nature, *To do as we would be done Unto.* It's therefore the Publick Welfare and Safety, requires more Circumſpection and Care, to prevent its being Impoſed upon now-a-days than ever before; for that natural Simplicity, which ought to be adherent to Probity and Honeſty, is no more in Being. Sharping, and Out-witting, have now the Preheminence, eſpecially when its well known, That the Perſon, whoſe Talents were always employed for the Ruin of the Publick, to advance his own and others private Intereſt, and which Perſon, and his Inventions, makes ſo many Honeſt Men, Widows, and Orphans, Sigh, and ſhed Tears to Heaven to this Day, Witneſs, a whole Neighbouring-Kingdom, and his being the leading Card to the misfortunes of the *South-Sea*, is now actually at the

the Court of *Great-Britain*, and without Doubt, at the Bottom of Mr. *Wood's* Affair, in Order to make *Ireland* partake in the Curſe he brought elſewhere, for he cannot be at quiet any where. This Anſwers ſufficiently the Objection made, why the People of *Ireland*, ſhould uſe more Precaution now than they did in reference to the Patents Granted, in King *Charles*, and King *James's*, &c. their Time. Now as to the Argument made uſe of, for inducing his Majeſty to confirm Mr. *Wood's* Patent, That the Lord Lieutenant of *Ireland*, or the Lords Juſtices and Council upon the repeated Orders of his Majeſty, would not ſrnd over ſuch Perſons as may be proper, to make good, or ſupport the Objections made againſt ſaid Patent, or Patentee, their Reaſons for not complying, being at the ſame time ſpecified ; ſufficiently reſolve the matter, for there its ſaid, That the Lord Lieutenant upon Conſulting the Chief Members of both Houſes, who were immediately in His Majeſty's Service, and of the Privy Council of *Ireland*, *That none of them would take upon them, to adviſe how any material Perſons, or Papers, might be ſent over upon this Occaſion, That they all ſeemed apprehenſive of the ill Temper, any miſcarriage in a Tryal upon* Scire Facias *brought againſt the Patentee, might Occaſion in both Houſes of Parliament in* Ireland, *if the Evidence were not laid as full before a Jury in* London ; *as it was before ſaid Houſes in* Ireland, *and that the Lord Lieutenant did therefore a Second Time, Decline ſending over any Perſons, Papers, or Materials whatſoever, to ſupport ſaid Charge, brought againſt ſaid Patent, or Patentee, by both ſaid Houſes of Parliament.* And

And in another Letter in Anſwer to theſe Orders of his Majeſty; Dated the 23*d* of *April* laſt: The Lord Lieutenant ſays, that in order to obey His Majeſty's Command, as far as Poſſibly he could; at a Meeting with the Lord Chancellor, the Chief Judges, His Majeſty's Attorney and Sollicitor-General, he had earneſtly deſired their Advice and Aſſiſtance, to Enable him to ſend over ſuch Witneſſes as might be neceſſary to ſupport the Charge againſt Mr. *Wood*'s Patent, and the Execution thereof. That the reſult of ſaid Meeting, was ſuch, that the Lord Lieutenant could not reap the leaſt Advantage or Aſſiſtance from it: *Every one being ſo guarded with Caution, againſt giving any Advice or Opinion in this matter of State, apprehending great danger to themſelves, from medling in it.*

Now after ſuch Declarations from the Chief Members of the Parliament of *Ireland*, who were of the Privy Council, and of the Lord Chancellor, the Chief Judges, and His Majeſty's Attorney and Sollicitor-General. It ought not to ſeem ſtrange, that no Perſons who had already given their Evidence before the Parliament of *Ireland*; and of the truth of which Evidence the ſaid Parliament Declared themſelves fully convinced and ſatisfied, as by their Addreſſes to His Majeſty appears. I ſay that ſuch Evidence or Perſons were not ſent from *Ireland*; and that very well for fear of a Miſcarriage in an inquiry before His Majeſty, or in a Proceeding by due Courſe of Law in ſaid Caſe ought not to ſeem ſtrange, for how could ſaid Members of both ſaid Houſes, in caſe of ſaid Miſcarriage Anſwer

ſuch

ſuch Proceedings to both ſaid Houſes, or that they ſhould aſſume the Liberty of bringing in Reviſion, an Affair ſo Solemnly decided by both ſaid Houſes already, and that ſuch Miſcarriage might very well be apprehended is Evident ; ſeeing, that upon a Denial ſo well grounded, another Method is taken to ſupport ſaid Patent, *viz.* upon making an Eſſay in *London*, of ſuch Specimens and Tryal-pieces, as Mr. *Wood* and his Friends, and ſuch as are to be conſiderable Gainers by ſaid Patent had brought from *Briſtol*, and ſaid Specimens and Tryal-pieces being found to Anſwer the Conditions of Mr. *Wood*'s Patent, it is Concluded and Reſolved that Mr. *Wood*'s Patent ought to Hold, in which Patent his Majeſty Covenants and Grants to ſaid *William Wood* his Executors, *&c.*

That upon Performance of Covenants on his and their Parts, he and they ſhall peaceably and Quietly Have Hold and Enjoy, all the Powers, Authorities, Priviledges, Licences, Profits, Advantages ; and all other matters and things thereby Granted, without any Let, Suit, Trouble, Moleſtation or Denial of His Majeſty, His Heirs or Succeſſors, or of, or by any of His, or their Officers, or Miniſters, or any Perſon or Perſons, *&c.*

This Power given Mr. *Wood* by ſaid Patent being ſo very Ample and General, and whereby His Majeſty Covenanteth, and Granteth, that no Suit, Trouble, Moleſtation or Denial, ſhall be given by His Majeſty, or any of His Officers or Miniſters, *or any Perſon or Perſons*, &c. How is this

this Confiftent with the Claufe, faid to be in faid Patent, *viz. without any Compulfion or Currency inforced, to be received only by fuch as wou'd Voluntarily and Willfully accept the fame.* For if His Majefty Covenanteth, Granteth, or Ingageth that no Denial of receiving faid Coyn, fhall be given by his Majefty, or any of his Officers or Minifters, or any Perfon or Perfons, muft not all the Officers of his Majefty's Cuftoms, Excife, Quit-Rents, and of all his Majefty's Revenues in *Ireland*, receive faid Coyn ; and confequently muft not all the Officers and Soldiers, of his Majefty's Army, and all other Perfons Civil and Military who depend of the Crown, receive the fame, and confequently all Trading Perfons, Brewers, Bakers, Butchers, Shoemakers, Taylors, Receive faid Coyn, from faid Perfons depending of the Crown, or fee their Goods taken away by force by the Soldiers and others, and fo the whole Kingdom become a Pool of Blood and Maffacre ; for it's Evident by all the Declarations already made by all the Traders, Dealers Bankiers, Brewers and all other Callings in *Dublin*: And whofe Example the whole Kingdom will not fail to follow, that they are fully refolved to ftand by the Sentiments and Opinion of both Houfes of Parliament, and the above Claufe without any Compulfion or Currences forced to be *Received only by fuch as wou'd Voluntarily and freely accept the fame.*

What the Reafon of this univerfal diflike for Mr. *Wood's* Half pence or Coyn, befides what is faid already ; is the common Notion they have in this Country, that *IRELAND* is an Eye-fore to to *Great-Britain*, as to Trade, and Commerce, and therefore the People of *England*, are very indifferent what becomes of the Trade and Commerce of *IRELAND*; or what Disadvantages or Disasters may happen it, or the Kingdom in general; and Mr. *Woods*'s Way of Proceeding, in this Affair, confirms them herein; for Mr. *Wood*, if he had acted pursuant to good Sense, when he had got a Patent for coyning Money for *IRELAND*, he should have repaired for *IRELAND*, and consulted the Government and People there, and taken their Advice and Approbation of what Coyn he was to make, and the intrinsick Value and Weight thereof, and have given the People the necessary Satisfaction, so as Colonel *Moore*, and Sr. *John Knox* have done, in which manner he could not have fail'd to succeed; and until he follows this Method, and calls in all what is Issued of the said Coyn, and puts a new Stamp upon all what's approved of; I am perswaded he will never Effect what he Aims at; for if the People were prevail'd upon, to take or receive this Coyn, for half the Value, *viz.* The Half-pence for Farthings, and the Farthings, for half Farthings, the deceit would not be the less, for he would Coyn then of less Value, and Weight, and Practise all imaginable deceit to find out the 800 *l.* to be pay'd the Crown *per An.* with the 200 *l.* to the Comptrollers, and all other Expences; besides his own and Parteners profit: But upon the whole matter, why not the Coyning of Brass-Money, as well as of Gold, and Silver, left to the King or Crown, as in other Kingdoms, and Countries,

Countries practiſed, and the Advantages which may accrue thereby, (which wou'd certainly, far Exceed 800 *l. per. Annum.*) In which caſe there was leſs danger, or none at all, that the Subject would be impoſed upon; for in *France*, they give ſixteen Farthings, or Deniers for a Penny or Sols; and in *Holland*, and *Flanders*, eight Farthings or Doits, for a penny or Stiver, and of which Doits, every one weighs as much as Mr. *Wood*'s Farthings, thus the People wou'd be ſafe, and the doing of Juſtice in the Government, or Legiſlature it ſelf, and. not in *William Wood*, or *John Law*; or *Jack a Stile*, for I am perſwaded that His Majeſty and Miniſters, upon a mature Deliberation for the Sake of 800 *l. per. Annum*, will not give occaſion to this whole Nation, to complain to that degree, as may put it to Extremities; ſeeing the fatal Conſequences which muſt follow the Meaſures taken in Reference to ſaid Patent or Coyn, for its very well to be ſuppoſed how diſagreable it muſt be to this whole Nation, that more regard ſhould be had for Specimens or Tryal-Pieces produced by Mr. *Wood*, or thoſe concerned with him in ſaid Affair, and which Tryal-Pieces are ſo Evidently contrary and Different from the Coyn he has already Utter'd and Paſs'd in this Kingdom, as both Houſes of Parliament of *Ireland*, after due Information, Proofs and Evidences taken, do affirm, I ſay, That more Regard ſhould be had for Mr. *Wood* (the Party concerned) and his Contrivance, than for the Addreſſes, Affirmations, and humble Requeſts of the Body of a whole Nation in Parliament Aſſembled;

ſembled ; and that at a time when ſaid Parliament by an Eight Months Prorogation, was bar'd of giving His Majeſty's farther Satisfaction in Reference to the ſaid Affair, is what puts the whole Nation in a Fermentation ; and makes them Conclude, That Mr. *Wood* and his Patent is back'd or ſupported by ſome, who are no Friends of the *Iriſh* Nation, for they are already but too ſenſible of their Misfortunes only, by being ſeparated from *Great-Britain*, by a little Traject of Sea, of 6 or 7 hours Sailing ; That they may not have that benefit of Trade and Commerce through the World, as *Great-Britain* has, nay what was granted lately to a Part of His Majeſty's Dominions, to whom they think themſelves no way Inferior, nor leſs Faithful nor True to His Majeſty, and the Preſent Conſtitution in Church and State. It's therefore, they cannot but be ſorry for their Fate, That ſo little a Space or Diſtance, ſhould deprive them of that Benefit, which all Nations generally Enjoy, the ſending their own Manufactures to Foreign Countries ; for they find that little Toleration they of late had, of ſending ſome Woollen-Manufactures for *Portugal* and *Spain*, is like to be Retrench'd as well as all Trade is with the *Weſt-Indies*, without touching in *England*, and which proves often more Fatal and Chargable to them, than the whole Voyage for the *Weſt-Indies* ; it's therefore the whole *Iriſh* Nation could wiſh, That they might be alſo conſider'd, as *Scotland* now is, whereby they might no longer be under that Imputation of being Prejudicial to the

Trade

Trade and Commerce of *Great-Britain*, and not different from them in Point of Intereſt, Commerce, Truth or Loyalty to their Prince ; they Ambitioning nothing more than, That they might Exert themſelves as to their Loyalty for their Prince, as being Unanimouſly perſwaded ; They cannot be happier, than under the beſt of Princes, and far from the Thoughts, let what will happen, of Coveting to be under the Wings or Protection of any other Government in the World ; Their Religion, Liberties, and Properties, being not ſecure in Conjunction with *France* and *Spain*, or either, Witneſs the *French*, their Severe Proceedings againſt their own Fellow-Country-Men, as being Proteſtants, and the *Spaniſh* Bloody and Barbarous *Inquiſition.* And as for the *Popiſh* Party in *Ireland*, They, and their Fathers have pay'd ſo Dearly for Adhering to *France*, in the late King *Jame*'s Time, and have experienced ſo well the little Truth, or Faith, which is to be found in the *French* Court ; That they will not Eaſily be brought ſo far the Second Time. And certainly it cannot be well thought, that *Ireland*, or the People ſhould be ſo void of Senſe, as to have a thought to ſet up a Government of their own, in Oppoſition to *Great-Britain.*

Having no Power by Sea or Land, that could admit of any hopes of Succeſs, were it not better then, That both Kingdoms were United in Hearts, Hands, Trade, and Commerce, and that they no longer ſhould be oblig'd, to hear that diſagreeable ſaying, That the ſupport of the State and

and Crown, both in Peace and War; being only to be expected from the Power of *Great-Britain*, both by Sea and Land: Its absolutely necessary, That its Trade, Commerce, and Advantages, should be supported in Prejudice of any other His Majesty's Dominions. *Ireland* being willing (in Case of an Union) to be consider'd upon the same Foot, and in every Respect proportionable to *Great-Britain*; and thus all Animosities, Fears, and Jealousies, would come to cease, for what are the considerable Inhabitants of *Ireland* at present, but Originally *English*, and can it be supposed, but that they have a natural Inclination for their Native Country; if their Interest were but United, its what I heartily wish, for the Glory of His Majesty King *GEORGE*, for whom I wou'd Sacrifice a Thousand Lives, if I had them, and of which I hope his Majesty is perswaded, and for the Peace, Unity, Tranquility, Concord, and Strength of both Nations.

N. B. This whole Scheme of Copper-Money, is exactly the same as that of *John Laws Missippissy* Company, Notes, or Actions in *France*; for he made Notes or Actions, for so many Thousands of Pounds, or Livres, at such a Value, and which passed in *France*, for so much Currant-Money; so when the Regent of *France* found they passed Courant, and were bringing all the Silver and Gold into his Coffers, he Doubles and Trebles the Number, or Quantity of said Notes, or Actions, until he got all the Silver and Gold, and then they fell to nothing, and the People had nothing but Paper left, and just so it would be in *Ireland*, after all the Old Brass-

Kettles

Kettles and Pans of the Three Kingdoms ; were turned to Half-pence *in Holes, and Corners, in a Clandeſtine way, and nothing elſe left in the Kingdom* ; *Ireland* may then prefer a Bill in *Chancery* againſt *William Wood*, when he is marched off, like ſaid *John Law*, out of *France*, and *Robert Knight*, out of *Great-Britain* : All which Evidently ſheweth whoſe Scheme this of *William Wood's* is ; but I hope he will be met with at laſt, and get his due, not only for Murdering the Poor Coward *Wilſon*, (for Killing a known Coward, cannot be deemed otherwiſe) and Ruining ſo many Thouſands of Honeſt Men, Widows, and Orphans, but chiefly for this Trick he has play'd *Ireland*, in Breeding and Fomenting a Diſguſt, and Diſatisfaction, between the beſt of Princes, and the beſt of Subjects, by Impoſing upon both, and upon the Miniſters alſo, for what could the Greateſt Enemy to both, or all, do more ; purſuant to the Politick Maxim, *Divide et Impera:* As if it were in the Power of the Legiſlature to confine the Coyning of ſaid Half-pence to 40 Thouſand Pounds, whereas its Evident and Plain to the World, That ſaid *Wood* can under that Notion or Pretext, Coyn in *Holland* alone for *Ireland*, above 200 Thouſand Pounds, and the intrinſick Value of five Shillings of ſaid Half-pence being but 20 Pence, and conſequently what muſt the Nation loſe.

FINIS.

A LETTER TO M. B. DRAPIER

Bibliographical note:

this facsimile has been made from a copy in the Beinecke Library of Yale University (NZ.Z724st)

A LETTER TO M. B. Drapier.

AUTHOR of a LETTER to the

L[d]. Molesworth, &c.

Qui te videt Beatus est,
Beatior qui te audiet.
Si tibi dent animo non impar Fata Sepulchrum
Angusta est Tumulo Terra Britanna tuo, Buch.

DUBLIN:

Printed in the Year 1724-5.

A
LETTER
TO
M. B. Drapier, &c.

SIR.

AMONG the many Dangers and Disadvantages which attend a Writer, there are principally two Things that deter Men from exposing them selves that Way, especially in a National Cause: either 1st. a natural Incapacity for such a Performance; or 2dly. *Self-Interest*, being unwilling to serve their Country at their private

private Expence. But you, Sir, being ſo remarkably freed from the firſt, have had more Honour, and a greater Eſteem for your Country than to be deterr'd by the ſecond. Your wonderful and ſucceſsful Endeavours to ſave a ſinking Nation from the Hands of ſo vile a Projector, deſerve more than the Thanks of a Kingdom, ſince their Praiſes, as well as their Ackowledgements ought in Gratitude to follow. The indefatigable and unwearied Diligence you have us'd, as well in diſcovering and expoſing the imminent and lamentable Dangers we lay under, as in clearing the Doubts which might naturally ariſe, are ſufficient Evidences to prove the unbyaſs'd and diſintereſted Affection you have for your Country: And if (as God forbid) this Arch Enemy had conquered, we might ſay with the Poet,

> Robora ſi Linguæ Demoſthenis æqua fuiſſent
> Non Macedum Graias Mars populaſſet Opes.

But to lay aſide a needleſs Fear, notwithſtanding your Example and Caution which are both very ſufficient, I have ventur'd to write on ſo diſagreeable a Sub-

ject

ject as *William Wood*, and tho' I have observed Danger, yet I must confess I can't apprehend from whence the Danger proceeds; for to use the ever famous Mr. *Molyneux*'s Words, *We are in a miserable Condition indeed, if we may not be allow'd to complain, when we think we are hurt; and to give our Reasons with all Modesty and Submission.* But were it otherwise, it wou'd not in the least affect or discourage me in an Attempt where I think my Cause is good, and my Country concern'd, and where I am fully perswaded, the true Interest of *England* is as deeply engaged as the *Protestant* Interest of *Ireland*.

It appears very strange to me, that a whole Kingdom shou'd be kept in Awe by so despicable a Reptile as this *Wood*, and that Men of remarkable Fortune Interest and Learning have been cautious of mentioning so insignificant a Creature. I hope *Wood* or his *Friends* won't call me to an Account for speaking so irreverently of his Name.

You have so plainly shewn how notoriously

ously that vile Imposter has strove to abuse us, that the Repitition wou'd be as needless as tiresome; But I cannot enough admire what a mean and poor Opinion this sorry Wretch has for this Kingdom of *Ireland*; For if he had not the worst that cou'd be conceiv'd of us *Irish*, as he is pleas'd to stile Us, he wou'd never have the Impudence to put himself upon a Ballance with our Loyal Nation.

'Tis certainly very wonderful that the very Air should change our Constitutions, and that an *Englishman* piping hot from his Country, should, upon his first Arrival here, immediately be chang'd into as strong an *Irishman* and as rank a Papist as those that Submitted to *Strongbow* in the Year 1172.

When the People of *Ireland* Submitted to *Henry* the second, King of *England*, it was agreed by a general Council at *Cashal* between the People of *Ireland* and that *Prince*, that they, *Regiæ Sublimitatis Authoritate*, should enjoy the like Liberties and Immunities, and be Govern'd by the same

ſame mild Laws, both Civil and Eccleſiaſtical, as the People of *England*. And in the Year 1216, in the firſt Year of the Reign of *Henry* the third, by Advice of all his faithful Councellors in *England*, to gratifie the *Iriſh* for their eminent Loyalty to his Father and him, That Prince granted them, out of his ſpecial Grace, *that They and their Heirs for ever ſhould enjoy the Liberties granted by his Father and himſelf to the Realm of England.* The Grant runs thus.

Rex Archiepiſcopis, Epiſcopis, Abbatibus, Comitibus, Baronibus, Militibus et libere Tenentibus, et omnibus Fidelibus Suis per Hiberniam conſtitutis, Salutem: Fidelitatem veſtram in Domino commendantes quam Domino Patri noſtro ſemper exhibuiſtis et Nobis eſtis Diebus noſtris, exhibituri: Volumus quod in Signum Fidelitatis veſtræ, tam preclaræ, tam inſignis Libertatibus Regno noſtro Angliæ a Patre noſtro et nobis conceſſis, de Gratia noſtra et Dono in Regno noſtro Hiberniæ gaudeatis Vos et Veſtri Heredes in perpetuum, &c.

By this we ſee that we are to enjoy the ſame Rights and Priveledges with the People

ple of *England*; and from hence it proceeds that the Conſtitution of our Government both Civil and Eccleſiaſtical is founded on the ſame Baſis, and grounded on the ſame Fundamentals; and whenever the Laws of this Kingdom are Tranſgreſs'd, the Laws of *England* muſt conſequently be violated, and the Offender ſuffer an equal Puniſhment, ſince Govern'd by the ſame Laws, and Rul'd by the ſame Authority.

AND as Parliaments (which are the Repreſentatives of the Kingdom) by the Conſtitution of *England*, are the Councels by which the Safety and Intreſt of the Nation are protected, and by the Conſent of their great Wiſdoms, what ever is expedient and Uſeful for the People which they Repreſent, is Enacted and made into a Law; ſo, in private Differences between Man and Man, Courts of Judicature are erected, wherein thoſe particular Acts ratified by the Parliaments, are the Rules and Standards by which the *Judges* muſt examine the Cauſes under their Conſideration. On this Account, in private Caſes, the ſafety of the Subject depends much upon the Impartitiality of a *Judge*, ſince by their final Sentence all is determin'd, they ought therefore to be Men, free from Paſſion, unbyaſs'd in their Opinions, and Steady in the Performance, never to do a publick *Injury* for a private *Intereſt*.

THE ingenious Mr. *Clarke* gives this Character of that ever worthy *Judge* Sir *Mathew Hale*, It will not ſeem ſtrange that this eminent Man behav'd himſelf, as he did in his Place, if we conſider what Religious and excellent Rules he drew up, and propos'd to himſelf to walk and act by in all his Employments, in the Station and Calling wherein God and his King had ſet him, which he ſtil'd Things neceſſary to be had in Remembrance.

1*ſt*. That in the Adminiſtration of *Juſtice*, I am intruſted for *God*, the *King* and my *Country*.

2*dly*. That it be done uprightly, deliberately and reſolutely.

3*dly*. That in the Execution of *Juſtice*, I carefully lay aſide mine own Paſſions, and not give Way to them, however provok'd.

4*th*.

4*thly*. That I be wholly intent upon the the Busineſs I am about.

5*thly*. That I ſuffer not my ſelf to be prepoſeſs'd with any Judgement at all, 'till all the Buſineſs, and both Parties are heard.

DIVERS other ſuch like Rules he ſet down, which for Brevity's ſake are here omitted. He wou'd never receive private Addreſſes, or Recommendations from the greateſt Perſons in any Matter in which *Juſtice* was concerned.

ONCE adds the ſame Author, one of the *firſt Peers* of *England* went to his Chambers and told him, that having a Suit of Law to be try'd before him, he was come to acquaint him with it that he might the better underſtand it, when it ſhould be heard in Court, upon this, that Great Man interrupted him, and ſaid he did not deal fairly to come to him about ſuch Affairs, for he never received any Information of Cauſes, but in open Court, where both Parties were to be heard alike, and therefore would not ſuffer him to go on.

A-

ANOTHER eminent Author gives this Character of a J——ge, That he excercis'd Justice in his own Time and Way, he never Befriended the Great to the Prejudice of those that were Little and Mean in the World, he ever held the Ballance of Justice in an even Hand, and acted as impartially, as if all that came before him had neither Acquaintance nor Interest in him at all.

AND they are expresly commanded so to do by Virtue of their Oath, made 18 *Ed.* 3, 1344, which says " Ye shall Swear
" that well and lawfully ye shall serve
" our Sovereign Lord the K I N G, and
" his *People*, in the Office of *Justice*, and
" and that lawfully ye shall Counsel the
" *King* in his Business, and that ye shall
" not counsel, nor assent to any Thing,
" which may turn him in Damage or
" Disherison by any Manner, Way or
" Colour. And that ye shall not know
" the Damage or Disherison of him,
" whereof ye shall not Cause him to be
" warned by your self or by other, and,
" *that* ye shall do equal *Law*, and Execu-
" tion of *Right* to all his Subjects, Rich
" and

"and Poor; without having Regard to a-"ny Person. And that ye take not by "your Self or by other, privily or apertly, "Gift nor Reward of *Gold*, nor *Silver*, "nor of *any other Thing* which may turn to your *Profit*. *&c*. And by a Statute made at *Westminster* May 7. 1346. 20 Ed. 3d. All J——s are thus commanded; "Ye "shall do Law and Execution of Right "to all our Subjects Rich and Poor, with-"out having Regard to any Person, and "without omitting to do Right for any "Letters or Commandments which may "come to them from us, or from any "other, or from any other Cause. And "if that any Letters, Writs or Command-"ments come the Justice, or to others de-"puted to Law and Right according to "the Usage of the Realm, in disturbance "of the Law, or the Execution of the same, "or of Right to the Parties, the Justices "and other aforsaid shall proceed and hold "their Courts and Processes where the "Pleas and Matters be depending before "them, as if no such Letters, Writs or "Commandments were come to them, "*&c*.

By this we see that the Duty of a Judge *is so Strict and exact that the Smallest Transgression from* Justice, (*particularly where the Transgression, is manifest*) *is not only a violation of his* Oath, *but also of those Acts of* Parliament, *which are made to* ratifie *it.*

But notwithstanding these invincible Rules, many Irregularities were committed, either by the wrong Indictments of the Sheriffs, or the Partiality of the Judge; to remedy which, the Power of the Sheriff was limited, and a chosen Number of Men, call'd Juries, were appointed to examine impartialy the Causes delivered to them. As 11 Hen. 4. 1409.——
" And that from henceforth no Indict-
" ments be made by any such Persons,
" but by the Enquests of the King's law-
" full Liege People in the Manner as was
" used in the Time of his noble Progeni-
" tors, &c. And the Power of those Jurors, by Virtue of their Oath, was so extended, that neither the Authority of the Judge, nor the Power of the Sheriff could oblige them to act in the least contrary to their Oath, or against the Rules

Rules of Juſtice. They were intirely independent of the Judge, and Sentence was continualy given after their Verdict: to prevent any Corruption whereof, there was a particular Penalty inflicted on thoſe Jurors that on Account of any Reward, or Benefit acted contrary to the Rules of Juſtice. As the Statute ſays, "that the "Juror ſo attainted ſhould have Impri-"ſonment for one Year, which Impriſon-"ment the King, granteth that it ſhall not "be pardoned for any Fine, &c.

It is entirely on the Duty of a Judge and Jury that our Safety and Intereſt depends, and the Obligations of Juſtice in both are ſo very firm, that our Fortunes depend upon an excellent Foundation; but if a Judge, contrary to Juſtice, ſhould limit a Jury-man's Power, and corrupt thoſe Laws, I know not how our Lives or Fortunes cou'd long ſtand in their former Security.

It was an excellent Obſervation of *Cicero*, *Quod nihil eſt utile, niſi idem ſit honeſtum*, but how much were it to be wiſh'd wiſh'd that private Advantage wou'd give way to Juſtice, and Virtue be counted a ſufficient Reward.

I ſhould now, Sir, ask Pardon for preſuming to write on a *S*ubject that you have ſo excellently diſcuſs'd ; but as you have not only deſerv'd, but alſo obtain'd the Prayers and Thanks of a Nation, I eſteem it the greateſt Honour I can hope for to have the Opportunity of ſubſcribing my ſelf, at this Time.

SIR,

Your Admiring Friend,

AND

Humble Servant.

Miſoxulos.

A LETTER FROM A YOUNG LADY

Bibliographical note:

this facsimile has been made from a copy in the National Library of Ireland

A

LETTER

FROM

A Young LADY,

TO THE

Rev^{d}. D----n *S----t.*

Presenti tibi matures largimur Honores.

Printed in the Year 1724.

A

LETTER

From a Young LADY, to the

Revd. D---n S----t.

WHEN Ought such Observation draws
To make a PEN assert the Cause,
When potent *Wits* with *Wits* engage,
And storm with inofensive Rage,
When Heroes brave, on War intent,
Rush on in Battle eloquent,
The wondering World with Praise admire
The Theme that could such Wit inspire;

And

And sure the Cause must be as rare
That can deserve a L A D Y's Care,
And make her *Tea* or *Cloe* shun
To turn a *Paper Champion*;
Tho' what can hurt or what destroy
Can never *Female Pens* employ,
Justice is still her glorious Theme,
What's Great and Good their Pens may claim.

But as a Young unskilful Maid
Swooning with Fear, and pale with Dread
Beholds her Love, with Tears of Joy
Returning safe from Victory,
With open and unartful Charms
Pressing the Heroe in her Arms,
Blesses the Dangers that cou'd prove
What Virtue 'twas deserv'd her Love;
So I, with Admiration view
Honour and Virtue join'd in you.
And bless the Time which gave a Theme
To make thy *Self* thy *Self* proclaim;
By this we see thy Virtues rise,
And mount majestick to the Skyes,

By

By this, thy Self in every Line
In all thy native Splendor ſhine,
By this, we likewiſe learn, tho' late,
To prize what's truly Good and Great.

Thus when the dreadful Din of War,
And Drums and Trumpets wound the Air
When Arms and embattled Trains
Of Warriours cover all the Plains,
(Secure of Conqueſt and of Fate)
To cruſh one weak and fickly State,
A Generous Youth by Virtue fir'd,
By Honour and by Fame inſpir'd,
Aſſerts the glorious Cauſe, and charms
The ſleeping Nation into Arms,
Honour and Glory ſtrait appear
And rouze their fainting Breaſts to War ;
All that before were drooping found,
Now animated with the Sound,
With manly Force their Weapons weild,
And all ſeem Heroes in the Field.
What Praiſes would that Youth attend,
What Honours would their Bounty ſend ,

To one whose ſtrong prevailing Arm
Cou'd ſuch a potent Foe deſarm.

Tho' in a *Different Cauſe* recieve
What *Praiſes* Gratitude can give:
Not that my *Muſe* affects to ſhew,
Her *courſer Thoughts* to *common View*,
Or thinks ſuch harſh untuned Lays
As hers, can celebrate they Praiſe,
But Pardon, Since by this *She* ſhows,
Tho' She brings little, much She Owes;
Wiſdom and unreproved *Worth*,
Need not her Skill to blaze 'em forth,
But will remain to *After-Times*,
Without the Help of weaker Rhimes:
Tho' others under Marble, plac'd,
Keep not their Titles Undefac'd.
Tho' Monuments themſelves Decay,
And lofty Fabricks Melt a way,
Yet Wiſdom's ne'er decaying Root.
Brings virtuous, everlaſting Fruit;
And they that Labour'd have, like thee
Shall live to all Eternity.

The

The *Principles* by which Men move,
Are private Intereſt, baſe Self-Love;
So far their Love or Hate extends
As ſerves thier own contracted Ends.

Hence as the Earth-begotten Brood,
Begotten, born, and nurs'd in Blood,
Which from thoſe poiſon'd Teeth, once grew,
Which *Cadmus* in the Furrows threw,
Within a While by Diſcord Slain,
Return'd to Mother-Earth again,
Scarce left a Token to appear
And tell the Age that once they were.
So bad Men vaniſh and are gone,
Buried in dark Oblivion.

But, THOU whoſe *more enlarged Breaſt*,
With purer Thoughts and Fire's poſſeſt,
Not Sway'd by baſe, or private *Ends*,
But ſtill the *Common Good* attends,
Can't unregarded paſs, Since *Fame*,
Enobles and perpetuates thy Name.
Thus who of *Old*, when Folly reign'd,
By Study or by Toil obtain'd,
Did to the infant World impart,
Some ſignal Benefit, or Art,

Had ſhrines preſented; hence Aroſe,
Ceres and *Bacchus*, Gods like theſe,
Wou'd *Piety* or *Truth*, admit.
Of ſuch like God's, 'twere far more fit,
For *Thee*, then thoſe who taught us how
To tread the Preſs, or hold the Plough,
Since this *Grand Difference* we find,
They fed the *Body*, thou, the *Mind*,

Oh might our Mounting Wiſhes See,
A *S O N*, as *great*, as *good* as *Thee*,
Like *Thee* in Wiſdom *blazing forth*,
Inheriting his Father's Worth,
In Joy then might *Hibernia reſt*,
And boldy ſay *I'm truly bleſt*,
Then might *She* laſt in ſuch a Truſt,
Till Braſs wou'd moulder into Duſt.

F I N I S.

THE PRESENT STATE OF IRELAND CONSIDER'D

Bibliographical note:

this facsimile has been made from a copy in the National Library of Ireland (6551)

THE Present STATE OF IRELAND Consider'd

In a LETTER to The Rev^d. Dean Swift.

By a True Patriot.

Dulce & decorum est pro Patria mori. Hor.

Printed in the Year, 1724

The Present STATE of

IRELAND

Reverend Sir:

THE ardent Zeal you have always been inspir'd with for the Good of your Country in general, nobly displays it self in all your Actions, but more particularly in your late generous Defence of this unhappy Nation, when the entire happiness, and future Glory of the whole Kingdom were even at the brink of *Destruction*, but by your vigorous Opposition to the malicious and destructive designs of villanous *Wood*; you have successfully dispell'd the dreadful Apprehensions, in which our senses were almost totally immers'd, An undertaking which has sufficiently prov'd its Excellency by the happy Effects it has Universally wrought on the minds of the People, which every True-Born Irishman ought joyfully to esteem, by rendring you ther grateful Acknowledgments for your timly Care of our Preservation. And as you have always had the Welfare of your Country t Heart, I must now beg leave in this to trouble you with my Thoughts on the present

sent unhappy Circumstances the Kingdom of Ireland, at this time, lab u under,

F r my own part, I am most sencibly concern'd when I reflect th t there is nothing more certain than that too many of our misfortunes are in a great measure owing to our selves, and the depravity of our Inclinations, who under a mistaken Notion of enjoying what the World terms pleasure, we too often disregard what wou'd tend to our Glory and Advancement, and by our Folly, pursue those things which have and do prove distructive to ourselves, and highly prejudicial to the Constitution and benefit of our Countery: For a demonstrable Proof of this, let us only notice some or most of our own Nobility and Men of Wealth, who to Enrich a most ungrateful Nation, not only endeavour to Ruin themselves, but even their Honour, Name and Posterity; for being unsatisfy'd with the Products of their own Country, they profusely spend their Estates & Fortunes abroad, which if impended here, wou'd enable us to furnish them with all the Variety of Pleasure they so costly acquire elsewhere, whilst their poor Tenants at home are wreck'd with extravagant Rents to maintain their exorbitent ways of Living abroad, to the Ruin of our Commerce, and consequently the impoverishing

ishing the whole Kingdom. This I take to be one of the most manifest and substantial Reasons which occasions our present Calamities, and render us Ridiculous to other Nations, who do not spare to mock at us, that we our selves should be the chief Instruments of our own Misfortunes, And I heartily and sincerely wish Heaven may be pleas'd so to open our Eyes, that we may be able to inspect into these Enormities, in order to their Amendment and the Establishment of our future Grandeur and Tranquility.

How many most grievous and dreadful Examples have we experienc'd of their undeserv'd Ingratitude to u, who have ever industriously endeavour'd to obstruct all our Atchievement, to Advancement by making us contemptible to others, and miserable to our selves; as if they gloried in nothing more than our entire Dissolution;

Not considering the innumerable disadvantages it wou'd undoubtedly bring upon themselves; nor the incredible Prejudice it would be to his Majesty, by the depri-vation of the immease Revenues he yearly receives from hence, which they must consequently make up themselves out of their own Fortunes, to their constant Disadvantage

D: ege.

Degenerate, unthinking People! who, whilst they aim at Ireland's ruin, are flying in the Face of our most gracious Sovereign, since thereby they wou'd destroy so many of his Faithful Subjects, whose constant Loyalty has been sufficiently prov'd, whenever Occasion requir'd, and I am throughly perswaded, that even at this time, when most oppress'd, they are ready and unanimously willing to lay down their Lives and Fortunes or the preservation of his Majesty and Crown against all Opposers. And how ungratefully are we requited! How unnaturally impoverish'd! and how unreasonably impos'd upon! when they still persevere in their immerited Ingratitude to us. And, so lowly are we reduc'd, that we are deny'd the Common Priviledge and Benefit of Traffick (the only support of a Nation) by their Prohibition of exporting the Chief Produce of our Country; nay, they have so far usurp'd a lawless Authority over us, that we are disenabled to redress our Grievances: And our once Noble and August Body of Parliament, as in both Houses Assembled, who were formerly invested with the Power of constituting wholsome Laws for our own Preservation, are now so far from being beneficial Representatives of the Nation, that they are become but meer shadows of it, since of themselves they are thought incapable of transacting the least Affair, without the Consent and Approbation of our Lawgivers, so that the best Use they can make of our Parliament-House, will be to turn it into a Coffee-House, where the Members may resort and talk of the Affairs of the Kingdom without the least Power of putting the most minute in Execution to our Advantage. Thus

Thus their voracious unreasonable Ambition is not content with the sole Government of our Kingdom, but they monopolize all that is dear to us, we are even deny'd Liberty and Property, the two greatest Blessings a Nation can enjoy, Blessings which they so much pretend to, and yet wou'd deprive us of the same Felicity: And so far are we discouraged from all kinds of Learning, that if there happens a vacancy in either Church or State even the most deserving amongst us are thought unworthy to fill it up without the least regard had to our own Countrymen, who have the only indisputable Right thereto, and who are daily rendering themselves capable of the greatest Places by their assiduous Studies and wonderful Improvements, since it is evident we have as bright, ingenious Men here as any they can boast of, but the many Discouragements they have met with of late has been so prejudicial to the Kingdom in general, that there seems not any Necessity for a Seminary of Learning here: And as a certain great Prelate was pleas'd to intimate, That the Colledge of Dublin would make an excellent Barrack since there was not any farther use for it as a Colledge.

Certainly any reasonable, thinking Person wou'd imagine these dire Calamities, to be Oppressions too heavy for any Christian Nation to bear that is in Peace with her Neighbours, and in the Possession of an indulgent Monarch, without the additional misfortunes of being impos'd upon by an insignificant, base-born Miscreant, a despisable, vulgar, knavish Varlet, whose unparallel'd Impudence has occasion'd the present Disturbance and Disorders of the Kingdom, to the great detriment of our Trade: whose Villany has been so happily detected by your incomparable Pen, that it wou'd be superfluous to say any more upon that Subject, but I must beg leave to add what must be conspicuous to you and every Man of Sense? for every circumstance of the whole clearly demonstrates, that this pretending, ignorant Creature; WOODS, is no more than a Tool, subservient to the Pleasure and Interest of some of the greatest Men at the Helm, whose Hellish Practices in the late South Sea Bubble (by which Ireland suffer'd considerably) sufficiently declare their being Projectors, and at the Bottom of this damnable Contrivance, wickedly design'd for the entire subversion of the Irish Nation, whose ready Specie, Exchange for Woods's Dross, was to have defray'd the Charges of him and his Abettors, and enrich'd some other Foreign Nation as heretofore: But, by the Blessing of God, and your Endeavours, I hope we have now escap'd their cursed Projects, ann destructive Combinations, to ruin our Country and alienate the hearts of his Majesty's most Loyal, Faithful and obedient Subjects. And as it is, I pray Heaven the Effects the bare Apprehensions of this detested Intention has already wrought upon the minds of the Populace, may not incite them to some dangerous and unlook'd for Undertaking; the prevention of which ought to be the incessant Prayers of every devout Christian and sincere Liegeman. Thus, Sir, having given a small Sketch of the present Unhappy State of this Kingdom, according to my Notion of it, I beg leave to subscribe my self,

Reverend Sir,

Your admiring Friend

HIBERNICUS.